Waiting for Good News

Waiting for Good News

Living with Chronic and Serious Illness

Sally L. Wilke

WAITING FOR GOOD NEWS
Living with Chronic and Serious Illness

All biblical references in this book come from the New Revised Standard Version, unless otherwise noted.

Cover and interior design: Rob Dewey
Typesetting: PerfecType, Nashville, TN

Print ISBN: 978-1-5064-3423-0
eBook ISBN: 978-1-5064-3424-7

The paper used in this publication meets the minimum requirements of American National Standard for Information Sciences — Permanence of Paper for Printed Library Materials, ANSI Z329.48-1984.

Manufactured in the U.S.A.

Contents

Series Preface

MY MOST sincere wish is that the Living with Hope series will offer comfort, wisdom—and hope—to individuals facing life's most common and intimate challenges. Books in the series tackle complex problems such as addiction, parenting, unemployment, pregnancy loss, serious illness, trauma, and grief and encourage individuals, their families, and those who care for them. The series is bound together by a common message for those who are dealing with significant issues: you are not alone. There is hope.

This series offers first-person perspectives and insights from authors who know personally what it is like to face these struggles. As companions and guides, series contributors share personal experiences, offer valuable research from trusted experts, and suggest questions to help readers process their own responses and explore possible next steps. With empathy and honesty, these accessible volumes reassure individuals they are not alone in their pain, fear, or confusion.

The series is also a valuable resource for pastoral and spiritual care providers in faith-based settings. Parish pastors, lay ministers, chaplains, counselors, and other staff and volunteers can draw on these volumes to offer skilled and compassionate guidance to individuals in need of hope.

Each title in this series is offered with prayer for the reader's journey—one of discovery, further challenges, and transformation. You are not alone. There is hope.

Beth Ann Gaede, Series Editor

Titles in the Living with Hope Series

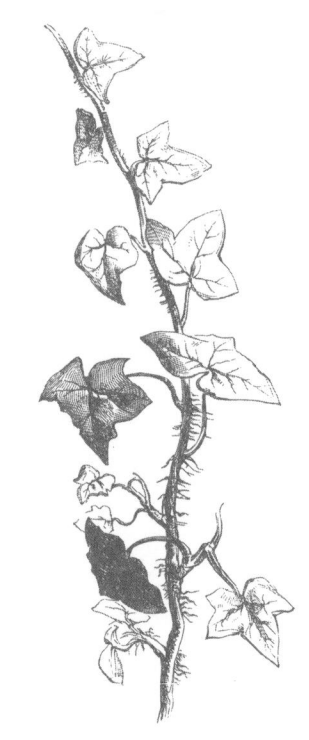

Acknowledgments

I AM so grateful to all the family and friends who shared their stories with me. I say throughout this book that asking others about their lives is important, but asking people to share their stories for publication was difficult. I don't want anyone to think that my interest was only to get words to the page. No one refused to talk with me about their illness or the condition of a loved one, although some asked for anonymity or changing their names. They, too, wanted to make someone else's life better and if sharing their story would do that, they were all in.

There are a few people to whom I am especially grateful:

My sister, Sue Kirk, who has always shown up for me with her wisdom, care, and amazing attention to detail, helped me put a manuscript of stories and ideas into publishable form. Her knowledge of grammar, sentence structure, and the contents of several manuals of style saved the day more than once.

Sue Drews spent hours of her topsy-turvy life sharing her grace-filled stories with me. I appreciate her authenticity as she talked with me in the midst of chaos, candid about both the terrors and the deep joys of her family's life since her husband's aneurysm.

I am grateful beyond measure to my kindred spirit, Beth, and my generous colleague, Brian, both of whom talked with me after the death of their loved one. Their candid responses to my probing questions were invaluable.

Finally, I am grateful to my family. I cherish the memories of my precious husband, David, with whom I learned, firsthand, what it means to live with hope. I am so thankful for the loving support of my son Alan and his family, who were affected in many ways during our life with illness. I appreciate the love of my daughter Carli, who struggled along with us and shared her story, and her family, who continue to provide a place of healing.

From the first marked-up draft returned to me from Beth Gaede, I totally understood why authors never fail to thank their editors. She was remarkable to work with and a challenge to my thinking. I wondered what she meant, initially, when she said it would be good to work together. I thought I did the work and she corrected it, but it wasn't like that at all. Beth is an amazing editor—she edited this entire series of books, written by several authors, but always gave me the impression her work life revolved around mine. I will never be able to thank you enough, Beth.

Listening to one another is among the greatest gifts we are able to provide and, in the process, we learn and are blessed.

Introduction

THE EMERGENCY ROOM was quiet until we entered. Then the lights came on, the questions began, and people rushed from room to desk to telephone and back again. Nurses and technicians came in, did what they needed to, and darted out again. By the time my husband was settled in a room, the fear was overwhelming. Each time someone entered his room, my stomach took a dive and my whole body began to shake. The tears didn't fall but constantly clouded my eyes. Each new test, every change in breathing, every alarm or bell, sent fear speeding through me. I felt like I could not breathe. The appearance of a chaplain or pastor immediately intensified my anxiety. Our life with serious illness began with internal bleeding that nearly took my husband's life.

The ups and downs, starts and stops of the weeks and months that followed were more like riding on an elevator gone rogue than a car trip though rolling mountains or even a wild roller-coaster ride. The prayers began before the decision to rush him to the emergency room and continued daily, often minute-by-minute, as we dealt with fear, questions, and discovering what we needed to know to live with his condition. There was more to learn about his illness, possible treatments, and daily care. We would never again be the same. My husband's illness changed not only his life but our family's life forever.

After a series of blood transfusions and treatments to stabilize his condition, the terror abated. It was several weeks before we received the final diagnosis. The hepatitis C that had entered his bloodstream more than twenty-five years earlier had nearly destroyed his liver and was responsible for the bleed. And there was no cure. Hope kept us moving and weekly treatments kept us focused, but the question remained, "Would his liver regenerate itself before he died?"

This book is for those of you dealing with chronic illness and pain in your own lives and for those of you seeking to provide pastoral care to individuals and families. Although no resource can meet the unique needs and desires of each audience, this book rests on knowing—no matter the situation—that all of us need to feel safe, secure, accepted, and loved. We all need to know we are part of something bigger than ourselves. And we need hope.

Let me tell you why I am qualified to write this book. First, I get it! Not your specific situation, not your feelings exactly, not your experience in your setting with yourself, family member, patient, or client. I have been where you are now—as a child, a spouse, a pastor, a lay home visitor, and as a friend. I have lived with and through the chronic and serious illness of someone about whom I cared deeply. And I have provided pastoral care to individuals and families in similar situations.

Although I am an ordained pastor and have provided pastoral care to individuals and families in similar situations, my personal experience might be the credential you value most. Much of the following information is wrapped in and filled with my own experiences as a child of a parent with lifelong diabetes, a husband with chronic hepatitis, and others' experiences with chronic and serious conditions. You will get to know and perhaps find yourself in those stories as they are shared.

One factor that makes this book unique is the underlying belief that spiritual guidance and acceptance is vital when living with chronic or serious illness. I've done my best to share what was meaningful and helpful to me, as well as to others with whom I've talked, without dropping platitudes or one-liners from the Bible as instant solutions for your situation. The people I talked with while writing this book valued the depth and breadth of biblical and other spiritual resources as they were sorting through and living with chronic or serious illness.

This book is filled with their stories, my own stories, Bible stories, and ideas that will provide you with understanding, guidance, and inspiration. Further, it contains tools, tips, ideas, and resources for reflection and for obtaining additional support. Each chapter concludes with reflection questions that may also be used for discussion with family members, patients, and groups.

In my attempt to respect the diversity of experience among readers, this may sound more fluid and less directive than you might prefer. If that is the case for you, just go ahead and take any of my suggestions or possibilities as directives and follow them, as much as they work for you.

The chapters are organized in the order that fits the way my family responded and lived through the illness. Each chapter can stand alone, so you may want to read as topics apply to your situation right now. However, if you read through this book in the order presented, you will see a complete picture of the individual stories I tell. The book begins with the question most of us ask when we hear a diagnosis of a chronic or serious illness.

Chapter 1, "What Is the Diagnosis?," discusses those first reactions, the sense of fear and longing for a return to the day before. The first days, weeks, and months following a diagnosis are difficult and do not progress in a smooth fashion. This chapter introduces you to several friends whose stories are told throughout the entire book. Their stories tell of the struggles they experienced, and offer words of encouragement and hope. In the first chapter, you will find overview information on the types of chronic and serious illnesses that strike fear in our hearts, as well as references to more specific information.

Experiencing and working through the emotional changes is covered in chapter 2, "Why Do I Feel Like This?" Growing to accept the diagnosis and all that follows is a process that begins with acknowledging loss and grieving, and it may be compounded by anxiety, depression, and even post-traumatic stress disorder. Many of the emotional fluctuations you may experience will not appear in an orderly fashion, nor will they be fully resolved. They can be addressed, however, and this chapter provides ideas for obtaining the help you may need.

Chapter 3, "What Challenges Will I Face?," continues with a description of three primary challenges faced by those with a chronic or serious illness and those caring for them. You may experience others, but the areas covered include the challenges treatment may present, the changing nature of many of your interpersonal relationships, and dealing with a condition that is not visible to others.

My friend Beth, whose young son had a brain tumor, provided poignant insight and assistance with chapter 4, "What If the Patient Is My Child?" Although the information contained in this book may be applied to a person of any age, parents of an ill child may have special needs. Here you will find ideas for discussing the illness with your child, assessing their ability to care for themselves, and ensuring care for yourself and your family.

Eventually, we need to carve out a new way of life for ourselves, whether we are dealing with a serious illness or a chronic condition. Several of my friends share their stories in chapter 5, "What Can I Control?" In addition to understanding that our love cannot heal or keep ourselves or anyone else healthy, we do need to create a new way of living so that we can have a life worth living with our situation.

"What Do I Need Now?" is the title of chapter 6, which begins by describing the kinds of help we need as our future with chronic or serious illness continues. I share my story of our reluctance to ask for help and the opportunities we missed because we wanted to be self-sufficient. Descriptions of the types of help available through groups and organizations beyond the medical community also include stories of those who used their help. In addition to a look at the benefits of spiritual care, there is also a section on how you might provide care for yourself. The chapter concludes with a list of organizations that can provide the help you may need.

Chapter 7, "Is There Any Good News?," invites you to see the ways people in a situation like yours have grown and developed new positive characteristics and abilities as a result of the illness in their lives. Each person I talked with was just as eager to share the ways their lives changed for the good as they were in telling me about their difficulties. If you long for hope and strength for each day, this chapter will be encouraging and inspiring.

Now, let's get started. I pray the facts will increase your understanding, that the stories will tell you others do understand some of your experience, and that the Bible stories will give you courage and boldness to live with hope.

1

What Is the Diagnosis?

HEALTH ISSUES can bring us to our knees. Most of us expect good health, other than the occasional cold or intestinal distress. Anything more than that is disruptive and distressing. We lose our energy, our productivity, and time out of our daily lives. Our convalescence is focused on what we need to do as soon as we are well again. We direct our efforts toward regaining health. We expect full recuperation and we are seldom disappointed. So, what happens when a healthcare provider says you will not recover?

Jennifer told me, "I was eighteen years old, a senior in high school, when my physician told me I had rheumatoid arthritis. I thought that was a disease for old people. The first article I read about my condition said I'd be in assisted living within twenty years."

This dim prognosis was too much for her young mind to handle. She withdrew from her gym class because even changing her clothes was too painful. But she ignored the diagnosis. Jennifer remained in denial until she was experiencing pain most of the time and was unable to lift her arms at all. "Can you imagine being eighteen years old and not be able to put on your own deodorant?" The sicker she became, the more she knew the diagnosis was real and she needed help.

Hearing that you will live with your condition or pain for the rest of your life is difficult. "I cried, right there in the doctor's office, when she told me there was no cure and my condition would not go away on its own." Jennifer also set out to get more and better information than she found in that first article she'd read. Learning about the specific disease or condition, the signs and symptoms of complications, treatment options and daily living protocols is helpful as you anticipate its impact. What follows is a sample of the published knowledge about chronic disease, chronic pain, and serious illness. This brief listing may assist you in gaining perspective on your diagnosis.

Definitions

The US National Center for Health statistics defines a chronic disease as one that lasts three months or more and has no vaccines or cures. The Centers for Disease Control website on chronic illness and pain contains definitions, descriptions, and names of more illnesses than I ever expected to find. Chronic illness includes many diseases: heart disease, diabetes, multiple sclerosis, muscular dystrophy, ALS, Parkinson's, blindness, traumatic brain injury, birth defects, and many mental illnesses. Only 25 percent of all chronic illness occurs in those under age sixty, and many of us will encounter chronic or serious illness in ourselves or those we love during our lifetime.[1]

The American Chronic Pain Association defines chronic pain as ongoing physical discomfort severe enough to disturb normal life activities. Chronic pain is debilitating, exhausting, and unending. Jennifer's rheumatoid arthritis, as well as fibromyalgia, Lyme disease, and lupus are chronic illnesses that often present with chronic pain. Most chronic illnesses are painful. Chronic pain can also result from back injury, neuropathy, cancer, gastrointestinal disorders, migraine headaches, and many others listed on the American Chronic Pain Association website. Although it does not end the discomfort, knowing that an estimated fifty million Americans live with chronic pain may ease feelings of isolation.[2]

"We were surprised to discover people in our neighborhood, at our church, and in our workplaces who are also living with incurable illness and chronic pain," said one middle-aged man, as he shared the story of his brother's illness.[3]

What happens when a healthcare provider says you will not recover?

More detailed, specific information about your condition can be found in recently published books and on the internet. Ask your medical care providers to suggest legitimate websites that could be helpful to you. Be cautious about exploring the internet without assistance or sound recommendation. Unethical sites hide themselves using familiar words and jargon and often promote a miracle cure at a high price. Several helpful sites are included in the listing of resources, found in Chapter 8, "Where Do I Find More Help?"

Both the medical community and the health-insurance industry have specific criteria to define serious or critical illness. Their definitions include the type and expense of treatment and care you will be offered. I have defined serious illness as one that may offer both treatment and the possibility of remission, and that also involves recurring hospitalizations and the possibility of imminent death.

Immediate Concerns

Unfortunately, not all chronic illness and pain are easy to diagnosis. You may not have found a diagnosis yet. As you see physicians and undergo testing, you may still walk away without answers. In many cases, the symptoms of chronic illness are not as readily perceived as other diseases that present with visible or measurable symptoms. If you are still searching for a diagnosis, see "No One Knows I'm Ill," in chapter 3, before you read any further.

Whatever the diagnosis, you can expect to feel physically and emotionally vulnerable. You may have multiple symptoms and experience frequent pain. The economic, social, and spiritual effects may catch you off guard. Anxiety is a common response. Needing to be alert to new symptoms, handling travel, expense, and the time needed for ongoing treatments are all additional stressors. These combined impacts may lead to a sense of futility in the patient and those caring for them. Whether your condition is listed here or

> We were surprised to discover people in our neighborhood, at our church, and in our workplaces who are also living with incurable illness and chronic pain.

medically defined in the ways presented, we all need hope. If you are looking for God's promise in the midst of your struggle, please read on.

My Life Feels Upended

Sue's story began with her husband's headache, which they treated with over-the-counter pain relievers and ignored for several days. Then came the bump in the night. A crash from the kitchen awakened Sue. She rushed downstairs to find her husband moving about in frightened confusion. He was stumbling and incoherent. Sue dragged Jon into the car for a rapid trip to the emergency room. He had an aneurysm that ruptured, and the doctors rushed him immediately to surgery.

Despite surgical attempts to remove it, the aneurysm grew and within three days caused a brainstem stroke. Jon had two additional surgeries and was placed in the intensive care unit on life support for three weeks. Relying on assistance from friends and neighbors to care for her children, Sue lived at the hospital for the first week. "I could see him for only five minutes at a time. Yes, I was terrified. I had no idea what was happening. We thought he was going to die. All I knew was our life changed in a heartbeat."

It is overwhelming and devastating to hear a diagnosis of a life-threatening or chronic illness. The first moments, days, even weeks and months following the diagnosis often bring rapidly changing experiences and a range of emotions. The responses individuals or families give when confronted with a chronic or serious condition are diverse, ranging from "This is something we will learn to live with" to "This is a tragedy that has destroyed our life," among many other reactions.

Whether you are the patient or a family member, you may be so shocked at the diagnosis, you may not even hear the actual words. Even when you are expecting bad news, when it comes, it sounds like gibberish. You know those out-of-body experiences you've

> All I knew was our life changed in a heartbeat.

heard about? It may feel like that. You watch and listen, thinking this is happening to someone else. You aren't sure what you are hearing and may miss important information. You may be bewildered and confused. Many people need to ask for the information to be repeated several times. A wise physician will invite you to be seated and give you time to hear and begin to process what is being said. If you have questions, ask.

When the doctor told my husband he had cirrhosis of the liver, our shock and puzzlement were immediate. "But I'm not an alcoholic. I don't even drink very often," my husband protested. Just hearing that word, *cirrhosis*, was enough to send us both into turmoil. The doctor was wrong, I insisted. Yet I wondered, "How could he drink enough to destroy his liver without me knowing?" At that moment, we had no idea cirrhosis has several causes. We were both shaken and scared. The only thing we knew for sure was that his body was experiencing the death of his liver. Yesterday was over and today was very different. We needed to get some facts.

Everything you have taken for granted up to this time may change. You feel like your life has come to a screeching halt. Adjusting to the illness and continuing to live as you desire seems unreasonable. Leaping to the worst possible outcome only increases the fear and anxiety. Before my husband even began treatments for the medical emergency that led to his diagnosis, he was anticipating a liver transplant and fretting about the number of pills he'd need to take each day if he did undergo transplant surgery. No physician had mentioned a transplant at that point, but his mind raced ahead and mine with it. "If he needs a transplant and doesn't want to take medications for the rest of his life, he will die."

Wait. Time to back up and address what is happening now and what we need to do in the coming days and weeks ahead. The effects of chronic illness are broad, impacting not only physical and medical needs. Emotional, intellectual, vocation, social, or spiritual functioning is also affected. Each needs attention. They will be addressed in future sections of this book.

The effects of chronic illness are broad, impacting not only physical and medical needs. Emotional, intellectual, vocation, social, or spiritual functioning is also affected. Each needs attention.

Maybe you wondered, "What is the point of life now?" You may take the bad news to its worst conclusion, guessing that your life is over. Life as you have known it has changed, and you cannot see any future but continual illness. Joni Eareckson Tada, who had a diving accident as a teenager that left her dependent on others for her daily care, gave her account in an interview published in *Table Talk*, a devotional magazine published by Ligonier Ministries. Speaking of the time following her accident, Joni said:

> Lying in the hospital, I recalled that just months earlier I had asked God to draw me closer to His side. Now, stuck in bed, I wondered if my paralysis was His idea of an answer to that prayer. If this was the way He treated new Christians, how could He ever be trusted with another prayer again? Obviously, God's ways were far different than mine, and, for a long time, that idea both frightened and depressed me. But where else could I turn? To whom could I go? I remember praying, "God, if I can't die, then show me how to live."[4]

Many people are confused about God's action in their lives. "How could this be happening?" is an early and oft-repeated question. Early prayers focus on "waking up from this nightmare" and pleading with God for a rapid and miraculous solution that restores life to what it was before the illness.

The most common question when bad things happen is, "Why?" This is followed closely by the more specific question, "Why me?" We turn our backs on easy answers, on those responses that are intended to console, but don't. You begin looking for reasons, answers, for why this happened to you, to your loved one, to your family. Is there some genetic condition no one ever told me about? Is this illness a punishment for mistakes I made as an adolescent? Is it someone else's fault? Why me? Nearly everyone I spoke with about their illness told me they'd asked a variation on that question.

In her early writings, Joni Tada reflected often on the writings in Job, an account of his experience and response to tragedy in his life. Knowing her days as an athlete were over and she would need daily care for routine tasks was overwhelming. In her first book, *Joni: An*

For I know that my Redeemer lives, and that at the last he will stand upon the earth.

> Why me? One of the first occurrences of this question is recorded in the book of Job, one of the earliest books of the Bible to be written. "Why did I not die at birth, come forth from the womb and expire?" (Job 3:11). He continues with four more questions: "Why were there knees to receive me, or breasts for me to suck?" (v. 12); "Or why was I not buried like a stillborn child, like an infant that never sees the light?" (v. 16); "Why is light given to one in misery, and life to the bitter in soul?" (v. 20); and "Why is light given to one who cannot see the way, whom God has fenced in?" (v. 23). He continues with questions and complaints until Job 19:25, when he is finally able to say, "For I know that my Redeemer lives, and that at the last he will stand upon the earth."

Incredible Story, she described how some of her friends were like those who questioned Job in his difficulties.[5] As Job sought to trust God's love during his struggle, his visitors continued to insist that Job's own behavior was causing God's wrath and Job's pain. This type of response became confusing and added to his struggle rather than relieved the pressure. For Joni, however, reading the Scripture verses her friends suggested led her to a new question, "Why not me?" She cast a new spin on her chronic condition that impacted not only her life but thousands of others as well, as she later began her ministry, Joni and Friends, for people with disabilities.

Others wrestle with the idea that God has abandoned them in their situation. Karen, who was recently diagnosed with a chronic and life-threatening lung disease, told me how a favorite Bible story from her childhood—the story of Jacob's favored son, Joseph— brought her comfort. The biblical narrative does not address illness but does offer a glimpse of God's presence when feeling abandoned and alone. (See Genesis 39–50.) In this story, Joseph finds himself alone and probably wondering how God is going to help him. First, his envious brothers throw him into a deep pit, leaving him to die. Then they pull him out so they can sell him as a slave. Karen told me she loves the words from Genesis 39:2: "The Lord was with Joseph and he became a successful man."

When Joseph rejects the advances of the wife of Pharaoh's captain of the guard, he finds himself in prison. "But the Lord was with Joseph," Karen said, quoting another reassuring verse, "and showed him steadfast love; he gave him favor in the sight of the chief jailer" (Gen 39:21). While in prison, Joseph helps another to attain his freedom and extracts the freed man's promise to get him released as well. Does that happen? No. Joseph spends another two years in prison before his release and ultimate rise to power in Egypt.

Karen loves this ending and often seeks the good that can come from her situation. Karen said, "My illness is not my fault; my illness is not punishment from God for things I did as a teen. I know this, and Joseph's story reminds me when I doubt. Just as God cared for Joseph, I know God is fully able to redeem any situation in which we find ourselves. I am going to survive this."

Karen's understanding of the story of Joseph helped her avoid self-blame or the sense that God caused her illness. Many people continue to interpret their condition as God's will for their lives and either live with false recriminations they think come from God or look to their past for the cause. Those who have read Bible stories about illness and make assumptions about God's apparent response are traveling down a wrong road. God does not cause illness but does accompany us as we struggle to live with a chronic or serious condition. As Jesus encountered those with disease, he repeatedly had pity for them and showed compassion on them:

> Now in Jerusalem by the Sheep Gate there is a pool, called in Hebrew Bethzatha, which has five porticoes. In these lay many invalids—blind, lame, and paralyzed. One man was there who had been ill for thirty-eight years. When Jesus saw him lying there and knew that he had been there a long time, he said to him, "Do you want to be made well?" The sick man answered him, "Sir, I have no one to put me into the pool when the water is stirred up; and while I am making my way, someone else steps down ahead of me." Jesus said to him, "Stand up, take your mat and walk." At once the man was made well, and he took up his mat and began to walk. (John 5:2–9)

> God does not cause illness but does accompany us as we struggle to live with a chronic or serious condition.

We don't know if Jesus healed any of the others who were lying there, but this story assures us that while Jesus has compassion and does heal, there are others who may continue to live with their chronic conditions.

The Struggle to Understand

For the longest time, in my youth, I gratefully accepted and believed, "God probably allowed this to prevent something worse from happening." After a time, that failed to keep me from posing the question again and I sought a better explanation. When my dad died, I couldn't understand why a man of sixty-three would get sick enough to die. The response to my "Why?" question that I believed for a short time was, "Dad just wasn't the kind of man who could be happy in retirement. This was better for him." After that, I began wondering about God's failure to provide a miracle. When the *Challenger* exploded, in 1986, I prayed God would just put it back together again and was comforted by the excuse that "people would never believe it was God's miracle anyway." By September 11, 2001, I had stopped looking for the answer to my question and knew that God was present for those who died, those who dug, and those who survived. When I watched David die, my old beliefs came back for less than a minute. I caught myself thinking, "God could still rescue him." Once that moment passed, I gave David and myself into God's safe keeping. With the exception of the time I was angry that I no longer had my husband, I have trusted God's care, and my faith in God's unrelenting love gives me courage.

When it is too hard to recall all the ways God's promises have been kept in my own life, I turn to the Bible stories of God providing safety, pulling people out of danger, and rescuing even those some might think don't deserve God's care. I read the stories of Abraham and Sarah, and Jacob and Isaac, noting both the ways they got into trouble and the ways God delivered them. And when I've read too much of God's instantaneous healing ways, I look at the people who suffered for a long time before their needs were met. Ultimately, the woman hemorrhaging blood for twelve years was healed. But she suffered with her chronic condition for a long time before that happened. Knowing God heals the physical illnesses of some and not all remains disturbing. And the questions pour out again. What does it mean if I am not healed? Who is at fault? What went wrong?

I still don't have the answer. In a broken and sin-filled world, bad things happen. Even if we escape illness, pain, or loss, sooner or later, all of us will die. Most of us, if we aren't already living with the darkness, will encounter times when it seems impossible to figure out the meaning of any suffering. God is good. God is love. Whether we are able to put ourselves in the place of Joseph or Job, who ultimately won during their lifetimes, or we see ourselves in King David, whose life was filled with sorrow, by God-given faith we hold fast to God's promises. We trust the resurrection power of Jesus and we rely on the Holy Spirit for guidance.

Few of us are able to accept our situation without questions or anxious response. There are those, however, who seem to be able to put their illness or condition in perspective quickly. After two surgeries, considerable pain, and signs of sepsis, Roger accepted his below-the-knee amputation as just another change in his life. "How bad is the loss of a foot when the alternative is a painful death?" He is eager for his leg to heal well enough to receive a prosthesis and therapy, so he and his wife can get back to their world travels.

Roger does get frustrated by the amount of time it takes him to accomplish what previously were simple tasks. Like most amputees, he deals with phantom pain. "I never understood that," Roger said. "But I get it now. The pain is real and, thankfully, not nearly as bad as my previous foot pain." He is not happy about using a wheelchair for several months and being grounded from flight by his physician. He and his wife have made adaptations and continue to travel by car and continue many of the activities they have enjoyed in the past. Roger is grateful to be alive and is looking forward to many years of travel.

When Jackson awakened in the intensive care unit of the hospital to which he'd been flown after an ATV crash, he learned he had lost one eye and the sight in his other might be diminished. Only twenty-two years old, Jackson is glad he and his two passengers are alive. "When I think of what could have happened, to live without one eye will be an easier adjustment than knowing I'd killed my friends." His limited vision is still new to him, but he was out of the hospital in less than a week and back to work on the family farm. Like Roger, he is looking forward to getting his prosthesis and training his remaining eye to do the work of two. Learning to live in a new way may be less emotionally challenging for Roger and Jackson because of the initial gratitude both men experienced.

Another common experience in this "life upside down" is the unpredictable responses of family and friends. You may receive gifts of food, transportation, and childcare immediately like Sue's family did. Or you may have friends and family with their own ideas of what will be helpful. Some are bubbling Pollyannas who live in a world that is not yours. Others are doomsday proclaimers and may be just as unhelpful as the over-optimistic in sorting through this major change in your life. Be kind to yourself and to those who are not responding as you expect. It takes time for everyone to accept, live with, or even understand the illness or condition.

Now What?

Many of us need to respond to the diagnosis even before we have time to stop and process all that has happened. That's what happened to Sue. Following his time in the ICU, Sue's husband remained hospitalized for two months. During the first few weeks, he did not recognize his family and spoke in disconnected and halting sentences. He received on-site rehabilitation services and learned to know his family and began to recognize former coworkers. He could not swallow, he could not walk, he could not meet his basic needs. "How can I take him home like that?" Sue told me she asked herself, worried she would not know how to care for him. When Jon was released from the hospital two days before Thanksgiving, Sue put aside her misgivings. The first couple of days, the entire family loved caring for him. They enjoyed the illusion of normal as they were together at home.

But on the third day, he started yelling at the children and cursing at Sue. His inhibitions disappeared, and his language and actions were cruel. Rushing him back to the hospital, Sue told doctors, "This is not my husband. I can't have him at home like this." The medical team tried different medications and sent him back home after a week. Because none of the medications had changed anything for the better, Sue discontinued them and allowed Jon to sleep as much as he wanted. "He needed rest to heal and I needed peace." Once he was medication free and had the sleep he needed, the disruptive behavior stopped.

Sue took family medical leave and cared for all Jon's needs that were not met by visiting nurses and therapists. For the next months, Sue spent her days performing the many tasks required for Jon's care and keeping up their home and family life as well as possible. She was so immersed, she had little time to think about what changes would be coming in the future. The family's only option initially was to survive the current experience.

Other first steps may include frequent trips to a laboratory and follow-up appointments with a physician. Therapy or medications may be ordered to provide relief or minimize symptoms. Before we could think about the ramifications of David's diagnosis, we needed to set up a series of appointments to repair his esophagus and prevent further internal bleeding. We were in such a confused state at that time, we really never understood just what the process or even the purpose was. We just showed up every week, for fourteen weeks, at the outpatient clinic where David was given anesthesia and the physician banded his esophagus[6] while I waited to drive my still-medicated husband back home for a day of recovery. It's not that we didn't ask questions. We just failed to clarify the answers.

Rely on a trusted physician and medical community to provide both information and care. If you require a new medical practitioner or specialist, talk with friends, interview potential doctors and clinics, seek referrals and recommendations. Be cautious before signing on with someone who promises simple solutions or a cure.

Learn as much as you need through recommended websites, books, and conversations with others who have been through a similar situation. Make the decisions that must be made. As soon as possible, begin to work through the emotional and spiritual ramifications of the diagnosis of chronic or serious illness.

Be cautious before signing on with someone who promises simple solutions or a cure.

For Reflection and Discussion

1 How do the provided definitions and descriptions of chronic illness or serious medical issues reinforce, complement, or change your own understanding?

2 How have you responded to a diagnosis of chronic or other serious illness in the life of a neighbor or friend? How was your response helpful or not helpful?

3 What might be helpful to you in processing the diagnosis? Are you able to provide that yourself? From whom might you seek assistance?

4 Do you have enough information to take the first steps? How could friends or family members help when you feel overwhelmed?

Getting the Information We Need

Talk with all of the people participating in your medical care to understand both the options and the recommended protocols for living with your condition. Be sure someone takes notes. If it is too difficult for you, ask a friend or relative to help. Ask questions, and don't be afraid to hear the answers. Imagining what's next is usually far worse than knowing what is ahead. Listen carefully to the actual words being spoken. In your own words, repeat back to the physician what you heard and ask if your understanding is correct.

Some of the questions we asked:

- What can we expect in the immediate future?
- What will treatment entail?
- What are the diet, activity, and lifestyle restrictions?
- How do we recognize a life-threatening complication?
- Who else will be involved in medical care and treatment?

2
Why Do I Feel Like This?

ONCE SUE knew that Jon would live, she was not as sad and began hoping for a significant or even full recovery. She returned to her job as a classroom aid, working with students with disabilities. Because she worked only mornings, Sue was home every afternoon to care for Jon and create a sense of normalcy for their children. Together, they focused on Jon's steady improvement and prayed for recovery.

Summer vacation rolled around and Sue was again home with Jon daily. "Summer was our time. Jon always took his vacation time when we were out of school. We took awesome vacations that always involved lots of physical activity. That first summer I came face to face with what we had lost."

Grief hit Sue with hurricane force and knocked her straight onto a rocky shore. She began to recognize those parts of their lives that were likely lost forever. She would see couples laughing together in the grocery store and leave her cart full of food to run to her car to cry. "I knew I would never have that again, and for several months I could not bear to see couples or families going about their daily lives together."

"Once I started to take stock, I realized I had lost my partner, my best friend of twenty years. My husband was no longer the man I fell in love with." Her grief reached a crisis point when Jon met with a psychiatrist on the day of their wedding anniversary. He was about to run out of his employer-paid benefits. He needed a medical examination before applying for Social Security Disability Insurance.

"That was okay. But when the doctor wouldn't allow me to come in with him or let me tell her anything about Jon, I was scared. As I feared, the visit did not go well," Sue said. Not knowing his mental state, the therapist had allowed Jon to walk to the restroom alone. Sue was notified, and they found him wandering down a hall in another part of the building. Sue vowed to be a stronger advocate for Jon in the future. Sue said, "The therapist told me that he was one of the worst patients she had ever seen. He would probably be dependent on me for the rest of his life." It was the psychiatrist's confirmation of what Sue was growing to fear that forced her to deal with her loss.

Experiencing Grief

NO MATTER how we first receive the news, eventually we recognize we have lost something precious, and grieving begins. Like Sue's experience, most of you begin to notice and recall all the things that are now lost to you in your present situation. Grief may convolute your ability to hear and understand what is happening now and what the future will bring. You may be familiar with Elisabeth Kübler-Ross's description of the "stages of grief" that occur when loss occurs. In a website comment on her final book, which was coauthored with David Kessler, Kessler says,

> The stages have evolved since their introduction and have been very misunderstood over the past four decades. They were never meant to help tuck messy emotions into neat packages. They are responses to loss that many people have, but there is not a typical response to loss as there is no typical loss. Denial, anger, bargaining, depression and acceptance . . . are tools to help us frame and identify what we may be feeling. But they are not stops on some linear timeline in grief. Not everyone goes through all of them or in a prescribed order. Our hope is that with these stages comes the knowledge of grief's terrain, making us better equipped to cope with life and loss. At times, people in grief will often report more stages. Just remember your grief is as unique as you are.[1]

No matter how we first receive the news, eventually we recognize we have lost something precious, and grieving begins.

On Grief and Grieving may be helpful to you. You will find it listed under additional resources in chapter 8, "Where Do I Find More Help?" Most of the people I interviewed described the following three primary responses in their grieving process.

Denial

Because moving through grief does not follow a tidy pathway to acceptance and healing, some of us spend weeks, even months, vacillating between denial and devastation. Although many people do move quickly past the denial stage, denial can inhibit the grief process from moving forward. When there is much to do, as Sue and her family experienced, denial can be a comfortable place. It was not until dealing with Jon's needs became one of many regular routines that Sue was able to begin grieving.

For some, denial is the immediate reaction to the diagnosis of chronic or serious illness and reappears as often as needed to cope with the dramatic life changes. For example, Jennifer's first response to rheumatoid arthritis was denial. Just as her fear of assisted living kept her from acknowledging her condition, others whose illnesses have a social stigma attached are also likely to pretend, even to themselves, they do not have the illness. Epilepsy remains a condition with a stigma, as do Huntington's disease, type 1 diabetes, and HIV/AIDS.

A mother of five, who was still able to live at home with Huntington's disease, said she would rather people think she is drunk as she tries to maneuver her body than allow her children to worry about their own future. Sadly, she contracted pneumonia, which landed her in the hospital and led to the unveiling of her underlying illness. Her children were as upset that she hadn't told them about her disease as they were about the lingering pneumonia. In her weakened condition, she finally faced the reality of her genetically transmitted disease. She and her family are still working through their grief, and two of her children have tested positive for the disease. She no longer tries to hide her illness, but her suffering has increased with the added burden of worry for her grandchildren. If

> Although many people do move quickly past the denial stage, denial can inhibit the grief process from moving forward.

your usual strategy for dealing with new information and change is to ignore it or deny its impact, you may need to take extra effort and the help of a pastoral-care provider or therapist to address denial.

Denial was our immediate reaction to the initial diagnosis of my husband's liver disease because of our narrow knowledge about cirrhosis. Our desire to view ourselves as self-sufficient survivors may have come from denial. However, much earlier in our life together we had developed a process for dealing with losses. David called it "Going through changes!" I don't know if it's something he learned as a child, but it was the way we labeled losses from the beginning of our relationship. Each time we experienced the end of something, we talked about the change it represented. We acknowledged what we no longer had while giving greater emphasis to the new opportunities awaiting us. While we were not aware of denial in dealing with our grief, our response did take the form of fear in the immediate danger and anxiety around the future outcomes of David's health issues.

Fear and Anxiety

Experiencing the losses that occur as a result of chronic or serious illness can cause us to lose our footing. We feel fear in the face of immediate danger and anxiety about the future. This, too, is a part of the grieving process. I struggled endlessly, it seemed at the time, to count on God's presence whether life was going well or not. I just could not let go of the fear long enough to rest in God's peace. As that elevator of experiences charged up and down, with starts and stops in no predictable pattern, my emotions and actions followed that pattern. When the news was good, I relaxed. When the news was bad, I was afraid. My husband and I would feel great when he experienced no symptoms and feel fearful when they returned.

The fear was often compounded by guilt, falsely thinking God would somehow retaliate for our apparent lack of trust. We knew better than that, but in a state of emotional upset, we temporarily forgot that God always stands at the ready with compassion and strength in our weakness. God knows how terrifying the symptoms

If your usual strategy for dealing with new information and change is to ignore it or deny its impact, you may need to take extra effort and the help of a pastoral-care provider or therapist to address denial.

David called it "Going through changes!"

can be and how relieved we are when they are not apparent. We did our best to cling to the promises in 2 Corinthians 4:7–10:

> But we have this treasure in clay jars, so that it may be made clear that this extraordinary power belongs to God and does not come from us. We are afflicted in every way, but not crushed; perplexed, but not driven to despair; persecuted, but not forsaken; struck down, but not destroyed; always carrying in the body the death of Jesus, so that the life of Jesus may also be made visible in our bodies.

I remain surprised that I was not fearful during the twelve hours David was in surgery for his transplant. My sister sat with me and I was able to talk, pray, eat meals, and even laugh as we waited. I knew there was nothing I could do to affect the outcome and was, uncharacteristically, confident in God's care whatever the results. Today I know those hours were a gift. Fear has gotten in my way several times since then.

Ten years later, fear kept me out of the Intensive Care Unit room where the medical team was performing every strategy they could to keep David alive. I'd stand at his side for a while, having a one-way conversation because he was intubated and could not speak. After a short time, however, someone would rush in or out or an alarm would go off and I'd run, terrified, from the room. After several hours of running back and forth between David's room and the chaplain in the waiting area, I learned he would not survive. I responded to the news with terror. The questions poured out of me, "When? How? What should I do? How do I do this?" My bursts of time in and out of his room continued for several more hours before David's physician told me his organs had shut down and he was on life support machines. Before he died, I intentionally ran my hand along the side of his entire body so I could remember how he felt. But the minute he was pronounced dead, I left immediately and escaped the hospital as quickly as I could. How I wish I would have stayed with him, hugging him, and touching his head and face, creating a remembrance of goodbye. I was afraid. I don't know what I feared, but I do know I missed precious moments.

God always stands at the ready with compassion and strength in our weakness.

Anxiety is another expression of grief and includes the unspecified fear of future events. When experiencing anxiety about the illness or condition, unrelated concerns may also begin to trouble you. "How are we going to pay for this? The furnace is making a funny noise; what if we need to replace it?" When thinking about the discomfort anxiety causes, these words from Jesus's Sermon on the Mount come to mind: "So do not worry about tomorrow, for tomorrow will bring worries of its own. Today's trouble is enough for today" (Matt 6:34). This verse was so applicable to our worries, and the entire section on worry (Matt 6:25–34) may be helpful in dealing with your anxiety.

The news may be devastating, the pain debilitating, and the condition persistent, but, as Karen and others have come to trust, God does not abandon us. In confidence and faith, Karen is not anticipating a miraculous healing but counts on the unwavering safety and security that God provides. She was able to let go of her fear about medication side effects and seldom has those vague feelings of anxiety about the future of her children. As for me, I often apply the words Henri Nouwen wrote, not about illness, but about a Christmas experience that felt particularly dry. In his book *The Road to Daybreak*, he described feeling empty and lost at a time of great joy. Feeling so out of step with his surroundings was troubling to him until he realized that "saying 'yes' to a hope based on God's initiative . . . has nothing to do with what I think or feel."[2] God's desires and God's actions transcend any thoughts or feelings I might be having at any time in my life. His holiday experience and reflection remain valuable to me whenever I deal with fear and anxiety.

Anger

As I read long ago, "Grief will always get you one way or another." And so I learned. Following my husband's death, eleven years after his initial diagnosis, I prided myself on my lack of anger. I sensed God was taking gentle care of me, protecting and guiding me throughout. But the first time I had to check the "single" box on

> Do not worry about tomorrow, for tomorrow will bring worries of its own.

my tax forms, I was furious. The first year after his death, I could check the "widow" box. That was hard, but a fact. The second year, my only option was "single" and I hated it. "I'm not single," I thought. "I'm married to David, who is just with me in a new way." I believed the federal government, particularly the IRS, had no business naming my status.

This was just shy of two years after David's death. Once I felt and named the anger, I unleashed my wrath. First, I became furious with the doctor, who had wept when he told me there was nothing more he could do. But that day in my emotional state, he became the villain. I wouldn't have had to check that (damn) box if he had done his job. Next, I blamed the hospital and the attending staff and was angry they didn't do the right thing. In fact, the medical team who worked for hours to keep him alive came to me in person to give me their condolences and then sent me flowers with a card each one had signed. But I was angry and someone had to be held responsible.

I settled down for a few days, but when I put my tax returns in the envelope, that box jumped out at me again and I was angry with my husband for dying and leaving me with no alternative but to check the "single" box. That rage lasted a few days, and I was glad there was no one around to witness my misplaced anger. Being angry with a wonderful fifty-three-year-old man, who had so many plans for the future, was so inappropriate. One friend I confided my anger to later, reminded me what I already knew: "David didn't choose to die." Our conversation helped allay the guilt I had felt about holding him responsible for his own death.

My final outburst was the greatest surprise to me and came during a spiritual retreat that had provided so many helpful and soothing moments. We had just read about Jesus calling his disciples and were to share our answer to the question, "What is God calling you to now?" Suddenly, I was livid. "God isn't calling me to anything! God ripped my husband out of my life and left me without a call." While others expressed shock and discomfort with my outburst, the retreat leader was nonjudgmental and very compassionate. She and her husband spent the next several hours with me, listening to me give voice to my feelings and assuaging my guilt about anger toward God.

Anger can be difficult to deal with. It is unpredictable, arising in me over a tax return. If it continues to fester, unexpressed, it can come out at unexpected times. I've answered the question about God's call many times in my life, but never before my retreat experience, or since then, have I ever responded in anger. I have seldom had difficulty revealing angry feelings—recognizing them in myself and sharing them with others, usually appropriately. Yet, if we've been taught at a young age that anger is wrong—especially anger toward God—it may be difficult to acknowledge and address. I misdirected my anger because there was no one and nothing to blame. Further, as you will read below, when we turn our anger inward, it can cause depression. If you find yourself easily frustrated, annoyed, and irritable for no apparent reason, your anger may be churning and need release. I had my friends and pastor to listen to me and help me process my feelings. You may need to look for someone to assist you if you sense anger is keeping you from moving forward.

Anger is a typical and normal part of the grieving process, and a necessary step, according to Kübler-Ross. If you read the psalmists' laments, you will find you are not alone in your feelings and you will notice the good news that God handles our rage quite well. After my initial outburst, as I became honest about my anger, I sensed only love and comfort from God. Anger may feel justified but requires acknowledgment, a way to express it and give it resolution, if possible. You may need to release your anger by venting to a good listener, journaling or letter writing, prayer and meditation, drawing, painting, washing the walls, or digging in the garden—whatever works for you. As with all stages and forms of grieving, it may return to you at times you least expect. Remembering how you moved through it previous times can shorten its duration and impact.

Anger is a typical and normal part of the grieving process, and a necessary step.

> ### Working through Grief
>
> Working through grief includes acknowledging the losses and allowing yourself to experience the feelings that arise along with the facts. Experiencing the pain fully and deeply is uncomfortable but is essential to healing. Journaling, participating in a support group, using a devotional book for people experiencing grief, Bible reading and prayer, and counseling may be helpful in processing the grief you are experiencing. Trust your own feelings. We may find commonalities with others, but the grief experience is as unique as each individual.

Trust your own feelings.

Unfortunately, what we often hear when we express our grief to other people is a profusion of comforting words—words we may not be ready to hear—from well-meaning family and friends. Most people struggle with another's grief. Some are afraid of saying the wrong thing or reminding you of something difficult (something you never forget), so they fail to acknowledge your situation. Trust me, people are thinking about what is going on with you; they just don't know how to respond. Others are so uncomfortable talking about painful emotions that they want to help you resolve your feelings. Many of us can recite the stock phrases we've heard. "Don't give up now, he can still get better." "Don't feel bad, at least she's alive. Be grateful you still have her with you."

Sue said the statement that hurt the most was, "Remember how far he has come since his incident." She was trying to deal with the fact that he had probably recovered as much as he ever would. Like many of us, Sue just wanted someone to acknowledge how bad she felt. As you are able, encourage both those close to you and your acquaintances to listen without reply. Tell others that if they listen, they will be helping you talk about the illness. Let them know you need to tell your story, share your losses, and work through your feelings, to process your grief.

Whether you are aware of the grief, or never experience more than one of the stages, your feelings and your needs are real and worthy of validation and support. Just as there is no way to avoid grief, there is no single or right way to deal with it. This is your journey and it will unfold in your own way. Two years along in grieving my husband's death, I thought I should be over it. I will always be grateful for the book *Widow to Widow,*[3] which gave me permission to grieve as long as I needed to.

Moving beyond survival to hope takes more than time. It takes effort. Whether using any of the ideas, strategies, or experiences of others described in this chapter, you need to focus and work through what has happened to move on with your life. Unfortunately, refusing to acknowledge feelings of grief can lead to other complications, including depression. Please give yourself the time, space, and help you need to work through your grief.

> This is your journey and it will unfold in your own way.

Depression: Unexpressed Grief

Sue had to return to work full-time after Jon's health insurance coverage ended. After months of caring for her husband, children, and home, and managing full-time employment, Sue's body stopped working as well as it had before Jon's stroke. Not just the occasional ache, but debilitating pain made it difficult for her to function. After a bout of flu, followed by bronchitis, and then an overwhelming feeling of fatigue and not being well, Sue's physician helped her see that she was already in a deep depression. As she was being treated for the depression, Sue began expressing all the losses she and her family had and would continue to experience. She read, she journaled, and she contacted others who were living with a similar condition. All those steps helped her to work through the grief and out of depression. She especially appreciated the blogs that would appear on her Facebook page, leading her to people finding ways to cope with a disabled spouse or friend.

Physical symptoms, including weight gain or loss, changes in sleep habits, or fatigue, are not the only identifiers of depression. Most checklists include the following: lingering and unexplained sadness, loss of interest in once-enjoyable activities, feelings of worthlessness, excessive guilt, difficulty concentrating or making decisions, and thoughts of suicide. If you experience even only one of these symptoms, especially thoughts of suicide, you need help from someone skilled in treating depression.

Over time, Jennifer experienced several signs of depression. Her medication was expensive. She felt well physically, but the emotional impact of financial stress left both Jennifer and her husband feeling battered. "We had to figure out how to afford my medicine and still make the rest of our monthly payments." The constant struggle to pay for the medication created stress and emotional overload. Despite being able to return to work, stress headaches ruled her days. Her husband experienced regular bouts of nausea and dizziness that had no physiological cause.

Jennifer's and her husband's physical reactions took a toll on their marriage. Their life together worsened after Jennifer's mismanaged knee surgery. Rather than restoring her to strength and agility, her surgery created yet another lifelong condition. She decided she was to blame and turned her anger inward and became depressed. She was bedridden for six months and could not work for over a year. Her husband continued working, so a wound-care specialist and other caregivers provided for her and her children most days each week.

Jennifer and her husband experienced an ever-increasing divide as she was less willing to talk with him, sharing only complaints about her pain and becoming irritable with her children. Her remoteness and negativity, combined with the financial strain of the medications and nursing care, turned their lives upside down. "There were so many days when I wanted to just tell him to leave me, because I was too much of a burden," Jennifer said. "But when he did turn to someone else, it was more than I could bear."

Despite her husband's pleas to remain in the marriage, she counseled for a time with her pastor until she was able to believe she had done what she could for her marriage and she and her children could move forward. She confided that once the divorce action began, she stopped going to church and returned only after she felt God's touch when she attended worship with a new friend. In that powerful experience, Jennifer realized that God had been carrying her all along and would continue to be with her. She said the poem "Footprints in the Sand" was especially meaningful to her during the long days of her depression and following her divorce.

Jennifer told me, "I believe everything in life happens for a reason. I am as strong as I am today because of my botched surgery and divorce." With assistance from a new physician, her healing body and renewed trust in God's care brought Jennifer out of her depression to a place where she could sort out her grief. As she worked with her pastor and therapist and talked with friends, she uncovered her bitter grief at the apparent loss of control in her life. Her powerlessness had been so overwhelming that giving in and giving up during those long days of bed rest seemed to be the most practical response at the time. However, she insists that even at her lowest point, she knew she would survive and God would give her the courage to keep moving forward. "This condition has taken so much from me," she said, "but I will not let it take away my entire life."

Self-blame often follows the "Why me?" question and may also result in depression during or instead of grieving. We move too easily from thoughts of unfairness and injustice, from the feeling we are suffering undeservedly, to blaming ourselves for the condition. Whether blame is imposed by oneself or by friends and family members, anger at ourselves can drain our spiritual resources, emotional energy, and reason needed to deal with our situation. Moving out of holding yourself responsible can be challenging, especially if you already tend to carry self-imposed burdens of responsibility. My brother-in-law found relief meeting several times with a counselor who helped him understand that there is no one to blame for his brother's death, including himself. Despite Jennifer's insistence that things happen for a reason, sometimes bad things just

> Self-blame often follows the "Why me?" question and may also result in depression during or instead of grieving.

happen. You can find help out of your depression due to self-blame and learn a new perspective by sharing your feelings with a trusted friend, pastor, or counselor who can listen well.

There is no scientific evidence that strengthening emotional health will lessen symptoms of a chronic illness, but depression can exacerbate the physical effects of the illness and cause illness where there was none. It was Sue's physical symptoms that first alerted her physician to Sue's depression. These secondary symptoms and illness in caregivers are common in families living with chronic or serious illness.

Although depression is common in both patients and caregivers, there are certain conditions and illnesses that often lead to depression. Changes in the brain resulting from Parkinson's, stroke, or traumatic brain injury may cause depression. According to the National Institute of Mental Health, depression is common among people who have the following illnesses: cancer, coronary heart disease, diabetes, epilepsy, multiple sclerosis, Alzheimer's, HIV/AIDS, lupus and, as with Jennifer, rheumatoid arthritis.

Once depression takes hold, the person dealing with it may need medication and counseling to find a new path to living with hope. Denial may be helpful in the earliest stages of you or a loved one receiving a diagnosis of a chronic or serious illness, but it can result in depression after a time. Although depression is 15 to 20 percent higher for the chronically ill than for the average person, it is not a normal part of chronic or serious illness. Depression needs treatment as soon as possible.[4]

Post-Traumatic Stress Disorder

Current research indicates that what some may call depression is actually a post-traumatic stress disorder, resulting from an emotional or physical trauma. Jennifer experienced both. Frustrated at the refusal of hospital personnel to listen to her concerns and take a second look at her post-surgical symptoms, Jennifer was angry and,

> There is no scientific evidence that strengthening emotional health will lessen symptoms of a chronic illness, but depression can exacerbate the physical effects of the illness and cause illness where there was none.

as mentioned above, initially turned that anger on herself. When Jennifer learned that a crushed artery during the surgery left her nerves and muscles without blood flow in her leg, she was able to rationally hold the physician responsible. A new doctor diagnosed the compromised blood flow as acute compartment syndrome and nearly cost Jennifer her leg. A second operation repaired the damage by placing a stent to keep the leg artery open and the blood flowing as it should. The surgeon left a large wound open on her leg to allow the swelling to reverse.

Unfortunately, the second surgery resulted in yet another lifelong condition. Chronic compartment syndrome requires constant attention to the pressure and blood flow in her leg. She was bedridden for six months and could not work for over a year. Jennifer's doctor diagnosed her worsening depression and the personality changes that followed as Post-Traumatic Stress Disorder (PTSD), resulting from the trauma she experienced following what was to have been a routine knee replacement.

Although PTSD was originally thought to be a condition unique to returning soldiers, the current understanding among therapists working in the field now includes any unexpected, unprocessed, misunderstood, or prolonged stressful event. Traumatic events may affect not only children who suffer abuse, neglect, and the frequent absence of caregivers, but also adults who experience overwhelming events, including the onset of life-threatening illness and other chronic conditions.

Jennifer's new physician encouraged her to get follow-up care from someone experienced in dealing with the results of trauma. Following the same protocol used with many post-war survivors, Eye Movement Desensitization Reprocessing (EMDR) worked quite well in moving Jennifer beyond the effects of her trauma and out of depression. EMDR is a recently developed, nontraditional type of therapy for those with PTSD. The therapist leads rapid eye movements by moving a hand back and forth for the patient to follow. While focusing on the moving hand, the patient recalls the

The current understanding among therapists working in the field now includes any unexpected, unprocessed, misunderstood, or prolonged stressful event.

traumatic event, then gradually replaces it with a more pleasant response. The theory behind EMDR is that the power of the negative emotions lessens and can be replaced with the positive emotions found in recalling a pleasant experience. Musical tones and passing an object from hand to hand are also used in this therapy. Jennifer's therapist used the basic hand-movement strategy.

When I was working with a therapist to explore my unreasonable fear of disappointing others, I happened to share the story about my father's insulin reaction the night Dad and I returned from a week away. My therapist heard more than a passing story. She encouraged me to talk about what had happened and the impact of that incident on a twelve-year-old. We both questioned just how traumatic an experience it was, but she invited me to try EMDR with her. As I held and passed two heavy polished rocks between my hands in a rhythmic manner, another common EMDR technique, I thought about the look in my mother's eyes and the blame I felt. I continued to move the rocks back and forth as she encouraged me to think of more pleasant experiences. Ultimately, I visualized a different look in my mother's eyes and heard her say, "It's okay, Sally. We've got this. You had a long week. Go back to bed." I continued passing the rocks several more times before we stopped. I didn't expect magic, but I did feel a renewed sense of both competence and confidence. It became much easier to work through my approval-seeking behavior patterns. To the best of my knowledge, there is no danger in participating in EMDR, and it might just lift you out of your depression.

I included this information about PTSD not to alarm you or to suggest you may have the disorder but to offer a road to help if you are experiencing severe depression that is not controlled by counseling or anti-depressant medications. If your anger toward God continues unabated or you sense anger from God, you may want to explore PTSD with a trusted spiritual counselor. Many communities have trained specialists in providing care that addresses far more than physical well-being. Trauma-informed care helps clients regain a sense of control and empowerment in their lives, addressing the psychological, emotional, and spiritual impacts of their or their loved ones' health condition. Obtaining help from someone experienced in working with PTSD, as Jennifer did, can help reduce the symptoms that exacerbate the distress you feel as a patient or caregiver.

Your experience may not include these emotional responses to the degree described above, yet emotional and spiritual support will give you the courage and self-confidence you need to continue processing your situation and begin to create a new life with energy and hope.

Activity: Using Scripture for Prayers of Lament

I wrote this lament, based on Lamentations 3, soon after David was first diagnosed.

Here's how I feel, God. Like you have afflicted me, driven me into darkness without providing a light. I know it's not true, but that's how I feel. It is as if you are against us, causing this illness and making us live with all this fear, pain, and unknowing. There is no way out, and I fear the disease will win and ruin me. Others have no idea what this is like, and I cannot bear their platitudes. Don't worry, be happy. Really? Be happy when despair taunts me and depression is all around me?

And you already know this. Because you are God and you are my hope. Your love never ends. You are always merciful and faithful. I try to have faith, but it is your faithfulness that brings hope and life. You know how hard it is for me to wait patiently for you, for me to endure this situation always waiting, always hoping. I know this; you do not reject me. You do not turn away and let me deal with my life alone.

Lead me in your compassion that I trust your everlasting love will hold. No matter what happens, you keep me close. You see me, you hear me, you know me, and still you love me. Hear my lament and give me peace. You are the God of all, the God of healing, love, and abiding faithfulness.

Now try writing a lament yourself. Pick a psalm that seems to express your concerns, needs, grief, gratitude, or any of your feelings. Read through it. Listen for God's guidance. Pray.

For Reflection and Discussion

1. What kinds of emotional repercussions have you experienced as a result of your own or a loved one's illness? How have your emotions surprised you?

2. How have you recognized your grief? What beginning steps have you taken to address it?

3. Where have you found help with the emotional repercussions?

4. How might your faith or spiritual beliefs help you to deal with your emotions?

3
What Challenges Will I Face?

WHEN JENNIFER'S first medications compounded her health problems, her doctor had to search for a solution that would help rather than hurt her. Fortunately, biologics were a new option for her. That was good news, but she still faced a hurdle. The new medication had to be injected. Jennifer couldn't do that herself, so she had to find someone who would be willing to give her regular injections of the medication.

My husband David also had to face side effects, but the solution for him was more drastic. In 1995, the only regimen that had any possibility of curing hepatitis C was injections of interferon. David's reaction to the first injection was nausea and uncontrollable shaking. We were frightened by his physical response and wondered just where God was in our distress. When his reaction continued to get worse, his physician asked for additional blood analysis and discovered that David's white blood count and platelets had dropped substantially. He was one of the few whose body could not adjust to the medication. If he continued to take interferon, he would surely die. After ten weeks on the medication, David's interferon treatments were discontinued, and we were forced to move on to the next option, organ transplant. No other medications would work, but at least we had another option. It was another six months before he could be examined, interviewed, and qualified to be placed on the National Organ Transplant Registry.

David was often acutely ill during the next year before his name rose to the top of the list. We were grateful that his disease was

Dealing with Side Effects

We had been so certain that the interferon was God's answer to all our prayers. I filled two pages of my journal questioning God's promises. "What do you mean, it will be all right? We thought this was the cure and the medication is only making it worse," I wrote. "I'm so scared," I continued, and then wrote this: "Don't be." Over and over again, we learned that we didn't just need to survive recurring visits to the doctor, the injections, the daily blood tests, the reactions, but that we needed to live day by day with God. Our hope came not from positive experiences but from the knowledge that God was indeed with us minute by minute.

still progressing slowly, but time was running out. He began experiencing brain fog, a condition that often precedes hepatic encephalopathy in people with hepatitis C cirrhosis. He was fatigued, irritable, and seldom interested in eating, and he had difficulty concentrating. I remember looking out of the bedroom window one day to see how David was doing while mowing the lawn. He was just standing behind the lawn mower, not moving. He appeared to be talking to himself. I was curious and went out to ask how he was doing. He responded with a gruff, "What does it look like I'm doing? If you could get all this noise to stop, I could get the fire built." Eventually, the fog cleared, the confusion ended, and I got him to come into the house to rest. This event took place just weeks before he finally received a liver transplant. His transplant was successful, but our life continued to be affected by the side effects associated with that treatment of his illness.

The Challenges of Treatment

One of the first major challenges you may face is finding and following up with the most appropriate treatment for the condition or illness. Not all treatment issues have resolutions, as Jennifer's and David's did. Most cancer patients, even those treated by surgery or newer drugs with fewer side effects, continue to experience

> Our hope came not from positive experiences but from the knowledge that God was indeed with us minute by minute.

problems as a result of treatment. Years ago, friends undergoing cancer treatments confided in me they were sure the cure itself was going to kill them. Some actually experienced life-threatening results. Others suffered from dizziness, nausea, vomiting, and diarrhea that was debilitating. Although great strides in medications have been made, chemotherapy and radiation still have side effects that can test the will to keep going. The treatments that don't result in bed rest, loss of hair, or severe vomiting may still impact the person's ability to engage in daily activities, although the drugs used to treat nausea and vomiting have continued to improve and are prescribed regularly for those receiving chemotherapy.

Several chronic conditions are treated with corticosteroids that decrease inflammation and reduce immune system activity. These treatments can be helpful in reducing symptoms and the pain associated with Crohn's disease, multiple sclerosis, lupus, rheumatoid arthritis, and many other chronic illnesses. Steroids work by decreasing inflammation and reducing the activity of the immune system. Physicians typically prescribe the lowest possible dose that will still be effective in order to reduce the side effects. Weight gain and a puffy face may occur in most patients being treated with steroids, but other possible side effects include high blood pressure, glaucoma, and recurring infections. The simple aspirin, used to prevent second heart attacks, may upset the stomach and create bleeding problems in some people. Be sure to report all side effects to your medical care provider so the dose may be adjusted or another treatment provided.

Whether the treatment results in additional symptoms or other illnesses, ongoing care can be cumbersome and difficult and must become part of the patient or caregiver's daily routine. Jennifer found a friend to give her injections of her medication when she discovered she was unable to do it herself. The father of a young girl with type 1 diabetes ensures that she receives the proper dose of insulin by monitoring his daughter's diet and activity level and checking her blood sugar counts regularly.

Just as we make adjustments and adaptations to live with chronic or serious illness, we can do the same in response to treatment side effects. The side effects may be brief as you or your loved one grows accustomed to the treatment, as is the case with many pain medications. The side effects may be predictable, as they were in my husband when he was taking the interferon, so you can prepare for them in advance. If you continue to suffer with pain and symptoms during or post-treatment, you might want to seek advice from your physician. You may need a different treatment, as David and Jennifer did, or there may be ways to lessen the effects.

Changes in the Family

When someone has a chronic or serious illness, or suffers from unrelenting pain, the impacts of the condition may be a challenge to family relationships. My dad was diagnosed with type 1 diabetes shortly after his brother died of the same illness. Diabetes is an autoimmune disease in which a person's pancreas stops producing insulin, the hormone that enables people to obtain energy from food. The onset of type 1 diabetes is unrelated to diet or lifestyle and appears to be caused by genetic factors.

Dad's diagnosis came at a time when people didn't talk about diabetes. Because it was difficult to control, diabetes was often hidden as a precaution against misunderstanding and discrimination that led to problems with medical care, insurance, and employment. During my childhood, Dad's disease was a family secret, and he lived in a perpetual state of denial. While he did give himself daily injections of insulin, he was unwilling to change his diet or lifestyle to prevent further complications. Mother took charge of his life by manipulating meal times, menus, and activities so his illness never had to be discussed. Although my younger sister and I had glimpses of the effects of insulin reaction, we were seldom given any information beyond, "Grab the orange juice. Dad needs juice now."

We could recognize a reaction coming on if Dad suddenly started crabbing about something that he would usually ignore. But

Just as we make adjustments and adaptations to live with chronic or serious illness, we can do the same in response to treatment side effects.

When someone has a chronic or serious illness, or suffers from unrelenting pain, the impacts of the condition may be a challenge to family relationships.

> ## Low Blood Sugar and the Magic Juice
>
> Low blood sugar is usually controlled by diet, exercise, and the right dose of insulin. Falling blood sugar levels cause jitteriness, irritability, exaggerated expression of emotions, and dizziness. People with type 1 diabetes often carry candy bars with them as an emergency treatment for low blood sugar, and when Dad could sense a reaction coming on, he would reach for candy. Orange juice, however, is much easier to get into the system once the reaction begins.

sometimes, he suddenly acted like he was drunk. One night, just as we were about to begin eating dinner, Dad jumped up from the table saying, "I feel like flying." My initial reaction was to turn and run away, causing Mother to cry out, "No! The fridge, get the orange juice!" Woe to the family member who ever drank the last of the juice. Once Dad got the magic juice into his system, he was completely himself again.

I have terrible memories of my dad experiencing low blood sugar as we walked home from church one Sunday morning. Neighbors gawked, huddled, and whispered. I was convinced they thought he was drunk. I also remember waking up in the middle of the night and getting out of bed when I heard my father babbling and my mother speaking very firmly to him to go to their room. I was just twelve years old and frightened as I watched my mother try to get orange juice into my father's mouth. When she looked at me as I stood in their doorway, I know I saw disappointment and was certain this incident was my fault. You see, my father and I had returned that day from his sister's farm, where we had spent a week helping with chores. Before we headed off to the farm, my mother sat me down and told me to be sure Dad took his insulin each morning. She also said I should prevent him from eating sweets or drinking more than one or two beers or Cokes while working. Dad was not part of that conversation, nor did he know that Mom had put me in charge of his health. "Remember what I asked you to do," was all my mother said when we were saying our goodbyes.

Somehow we made it through the week, but apparently I wasn't attentive enough. The scene I witnessed that night in my parents' bedroom was enough to set me up for a lifetime of trying to "get it right," so I wouldn't disappoint anyone or contribute to another's illness. That's one way my father's illness affected me. As you will discover, there will probably be both positive and negative impacts on the lives of your children.

Life changes significantly when a family member has a chronic or very serious illness or suffers from chronic pain. You may feel like your situation is a private concern, but the impact extends well beyond the patient and even the caregiver. Parents, children, siblings, other extended family, friends, neighbors, coworkers, church members, and others can all be affected.

Dad's chronic condition had far-reaching impacts, affecting employment, medical insurance, and self-care and causing frequent family emergencies. Ultimately, the disease resulted in kidney failure, adding a second chronic illness to adjust to in the last five years of his life. Dad was over sixty years old when his kidneys failed, and he was not eligible for an organ transplant. My fear of the unknown (based on denial and secrecy during my childhood) kept me at a distance from both his hospital bed at home and in the university hospital ninety minutes away. He was an early user of in-home peritoneal dialysis, and although he longed for visitors when confined to bed, I thought I was protecting his privacy by avoiding visits. It was easier for me to visit Dad in the living room when he was fully dressed, looking and acting well.

Are the Children Okay?

After Dad died, I realized what was so hard for me as a child. It felt like I was being required to keep a family secret I didn't understand. I think my siblings and I were charged with arranging Dad's life when Mom was not around, but we had no real information about what she expected. I didn't understand why my father could not care for himself. I worried about what was "really wrong with him," as if there was something suspicious occurring in my family.

For a brief time, as an adult, I wondered if my dad might be an alcoholic. As a prevention specialist and family counselor early in my social-work career, I was trained in alcoholism-as-a-disease theory. I was puzzled during the training because the family behaviors the instructor described were so similar to life in my family. Just like the families in treatment, my family also had roles, rules, and secrets. I remembered "walking on eggshells" and watching my mother manipulate situations to protect him and the family. My father had diabetes and he was not an alcoholic, but that training helped me clarify what had frightened me as a child and the impact of his disease.

I also know now how difficult it is to decide just how much information children should have about a parent's illness. Not revealing all the details may be helpful. When Jon was in surgery the first time (he underwent three separate operations during those first three days), Sue called their children just to tell them that their dad was stable and receiving excellent care. Loren, fifteen and a sophomore in high school, and Ethan, a twelve-year-old seventh-grader, were joined in the morning by neighbors who made sure they were cared for and sent off to school.

Eventually Sue wanted her children to be in the know, but children were not allowed in the intensive care unit. This angered Ethan, who came straight to the hospital waiting room after school. After failing to convince the nurse he needed to see his father, he quietly followed his mother into the room, where he was able to see that his dad was alive and still looked like his dad. Having their mother home nights and able to be with them a little more frequently was helpful to Loren and Ethan. It did not, however, diminish the children's stress and confusion. Again, Sue relied on help from neighbors, friends, and fellow church members. School counselors also proved to be a valuable resource for her and her children.

Our daughter, Carli, who was thirteen when David was first rushed to the emergency room before his diagnosis, was affected in ways we didn't see until after his death eleven years later. "When Daddy didn't feel well, he would just hide out in the bedroom for a day or so. Still, I wondered, why was he getting up to vomit so often, and why were we going to the hospital in the middle of the night?"

She said she will always remember our drive to the hospital when he suddenly fell over in the back seat. He had been moaning and moving around. "We heard a thump and then nothing." As she watched me white-knuckle the steering wheel, she was trying to figure out if we could just park the car and go into the hospital and tell people he was out there in the back seat. "I knew he was dead, and I didn't want you to deal with that. I didn't want to see him. And just as we pulled up to the emergency entrance, Daddy made a noise." Once she knew he was alive, she knew the doctors would fix him, and her worry went away. During that hospitalization, she stayed with friends, so I could be with her dad as much as possible.

Carli never accompanied us to David's treatments or doctor visits. Once in a while, she did go with David to the hospital for his laboratory tests. "I remember Daddy getting labs and how friendly he was with the staff there. He was always taking them flowers or candy, and they really liked him. Long after, when I needed blood drawn, I wouldn't be afraid at all, because they knew my daddy." While many of her memories are positive, she described how terrified she was before his transplant. "I used to think it was hilarious when you and Dad teased each other about the extravagant life you would have if the other one was gone. But now it wasn't funny. It could really happen, and I didn't want to live without my dad."

As scared as she was prior to his transplant operation, she was very relieved to visit him in the middle of his recovery. I wouldn't leave him until he was discharged, but Carli really wanted to see for herself that he was better. To save time and to provide Carli with a novel experience during this difficult time, my brother-in-law borrowed a small plane and flew her the ninety miles to the hospital. She remembers how pleased he was to be able to help her and how he made it a special time. Flying over our home, she said he told her, "There. Now you see what God sees when he looks down at you." She saw all the trees her dad had planted and the huge garden we grew together and felt assured again that her daddy would be fine.

After her visit, Carli stayed home with her grandmother, going to school, doing homework, and hanging out with friends. She told me,

> It was a good time and I could do whatever I wanted as long as I was home for dinner and in time for bed. Honest, Mom, I was never afraid again until the day I got your call ten years later to come to the hospital. I knew he was dying then, because he'd been in and out of the hospital many times before, and you'd never asked me to come.

A family friend picked her up and brought her to the intensive care unit of the local hospital, where she stayed, never leaving his side, until he took his last breath.

Talking with Carli, just as I talked with others as I wrote this book, I finally got her to tell me what was going on with her during her dad's life post-diagnosis. She says she wasn't always afraid because she buried her feelings, getting not just one, but two part-time jobs to keep her busy in the months after his first hospitalization. I pressed her for reflections and she recalled doing the same thing immediately following his death. Already working full-time, she added a night job so she wouldn't have time to think. She dealt with the fear and uncertainty by working, running around with friends, drinking and smoking—anything that would keep her from thinking about her dad. "If life wasn't going to be perfect, I didn't need to be either," she said.

After talking with several parents about how much they told their children about their condition, I was compelled to ask

Carli how she felt about what she was privy to during her dad's life. "I remember the classes we went to before Dad's transplant. They talked about the surgery, complications, rejection, and what to expect. Truthfully, after the classes, I understood less and was afraid more." There is no right answer when it comes to sharing information. Each situation and family is unique, and each of us needs to make our own decisions about talking with our children.

Partners and Spouses

Some of us are natural-born caregivers, and others of us are not. Okay, I admit it. I'm one of the not. Like our daughter, I valued David's strength and independence. On those rare occasions previously, if he was ill, he closed the bedroom door and emerged only to make a sandwich or get a glass of water. Suddenly that changed. Although he assumed responsibility for self-care as soon as he was able, I was actively involved in his treatment. He no longer hid out and had more needs than he could meet without my help.

Sometimes I had pretty selfish thoughts and desires of my own. David was a personable, outgoing, popular man and he received cards, gifts, and visits on a regular basis. I was often stopped while out running errands by people wanting to know how he was doing and asking me to convey their good wishes to him. After a long day of appointments and follow-up routines, he would relax on the couch and read the cards received that day. I would wonder, "But, what about me? I need cards and prayers too."

Maybe this wouldn't even come up for some of you, but wanting a little of the care and attention is not unusual or abnormal. Spouses of those who are chronically ill struggle with fluctuating emotions, responses, and added responsibilities as a result of the situation. I structured this book the way I did, so it would be helpful to caregivers as well as those with the illness. One major difficulty for me was not knowing with any certainty how David felt, physically and emotionally. He continued to pride himself on his independence and often failed to share how he was feeling. In time, he realized this was hard on me because I could get worried in a

> Each situation and family is unique, and each of us needs to make our own decisions about talking with our children.

hurry. Sometimes he thought his illness was more difficult for me than it was for him. As I was talking about my concerns one day, he showed his understanding by comparing my feelings to those of a passenger in a skidding car as the driver remains calm and in control. David knew when he needed to rest or to be active. He knew when he was angry, anxious, or afraid. When he kept that to himself I would remain worried, even panicked, like the passenger in the car. He began keeping me more informed, and over time, I learned to trust his abilities to monitor his own health.

In some ways, the illness became a third partner in our marriage. His physical condition often ruled what we could or would do and, some days, how we related to one another. This was not without its benefits, however. In the months prior to his precipitating illness, we had both been very busy with our own careers and interests. We had been spending less time together, thus less time talking. My journals from the year prior contain a record of my concerns and prayers for us to draw closer to one another again. Our deepening relationship is an example of God's redeeming power. I don't for a minute believe that David got sick so our marriage would improve. But I do believe God used the illness to reunite our spirits in a new and stronger way.

In addition to talking with Brian, a pastor whose wife had breast cancer, I talked to the husband of a woman diagnosed with bone cancer already in its final stages. Both men told me how it seemed the illness had a life and personality of its own. They spoke of times they were afraid of losing the ability to help their wives and other occasions when they didn't want to care. One of them experienced days of thinking his marriage was over. One husband described being terrified that death was imminent and times when he doubted his own ability to survive. When Jennifer talked about her former husband, she told me his experience was similar to what these men described.

All family members need support and others to turn to with concerns when a loved one is chronically or seriously ill. It is helpful for others to do all they can to help the one who is ill, but the family needs attention too. One thing I've learned to do since David's illness is to ask family members of someone who is ill how things are going with them. I may send cards to the person with the illness, but now, I also make sure I send cards and notes to the spouse and other family members. Readers will find stories of positive impacts on family members in chapter 7, "Is There Any Good News?"

Changes in Other Relationships

Your relationships will change because your life has changed and you bring something new to the relationship. Your friends, neighbors, and coworkers will respond and react in a variety of ways. Some will want to be helpful and will solicit your ideas for assistance. Some will provide perspective, reminding you regularly of what you are still able to do. Some will bring gifts and share their own difficult times with you. Many will provide opportunities for you to feel normal and to continue to grow into the person you are becoming. You may find those you have cared for now helping you. Some will share their faith without expecting your affirmation or gratitude. Some will be good listeners and encourage you to talk openly about your experience. Cherish those who have no expectations or suggestions about how you should live now. You may be able to continue those relationships, in a new way perhaps, but without feeling you are not giving enough in return.

Some relationships may not be as helpful and can bring unwanted advice or unrealistic expectations. Comments like, "If you would follow my advice and do this treatment, eat these foods, or participate in this activity, you could get well," are among those that cause us frustration. Some friends may believe that if we don't do what they tell us to, we don't want to be healthy. Being told the illness is our own fault can cause self-recrimination and unending "if only's." Some, who are uncomfortable with illness, may either doubt our experience or ignore our situation. It is easy for me to suggest you limit contact with those who don't or won't believe

> Your relationships will change because your life has changed and you bring something new to the relationship.

you, understand you, or relate to your challenges, but that may not be possible and you may not want to do that. Rather than trying to convince another, change the subject and move to a different shared experience you may have. Acknowledge their interest and offer to share the facts about your condition by way of a link from the Centers for Disease Control or the American Medical Association. You could try the blank stare, silence, or quiet smile and not respond in words. If all else fails, share your trust in your healthcare providers and inquire about the health of your friend. There are additional ideas in the sidebar included in the following section.

No One Knows I'm Ill

Whether the invisibility of a chronic condition is due to the lack of obvious symptoms or the patient's or family's denial, living with an illness no one is able to see can be exasperating. Nancy, a gifted Sunday school teacher, struggled with chronic pain. Chronic pain can be one of the most challenging types of invisible conditions. Unrelenting pain, without any outward signs, can leave the person in pain and their families struggling for validation. When Nancy's pain was controlled, she was patient, encouraging, and loving. Even with pain, her grace-filled love for Jesus was irresistible to the children she taught. Unfortunately, when the pain was severe over a long time, she was unable to function at all and received strong criticism for gaps in her teaching schedule. This generous woman would have appreciated greater understanding of chronic pain and love that was less judgmental and demanding.

While chronic and serious conditions like Parkinson's, paralysis, Lou Gehrig's disease, and multiple limb loss can be quickly perceived and identified by observers, a number of illnesses are far less visible (often resulting in people crying "foul" when a person with congestive heart failure parks in a space for the handicapped and then strolls, apparently comfortably, into a store). People suffering from these less-obvious illnesses seldom receive the level of understanding or depth of caring that those with the more visible conditions do. This is difficult for both the patient and loved ones. A great deal of exhausting effort must be used to provide the patient with the appropriate rest, medications, and supports, only to give the impression there is no illness. Patients and family members of those with an invisible illness get tired of apologizing, explaining, and avoiding those who fail to understand their situation. Their fatigue is a frequent and normal reaction.

Other invisible chronic conditions, including chronic fatigue syndrome, irritable bowel syndrome, endometriosis, and Crohn's disease, can cause unrelenting pain. Fatigue, which involves the entire mind, spirit, and body and is not the same as being tired, adds to the stress and disability of someone with one of these chronic illnesses.

Illnesses such as fibromyalgia, lupus, and Lyme disease were formerly diagnosed by a process of elimination. As these conditions continue to be more clearly defined and the diagnosis becomes more specific, they are less likely to be ignored or neglected. However, the stigma that attaches to invisible illnesses may remain. Each of these conditions usually causes intermittent pain and immobility, but the patient may try to hide it to avoid others' judgments, lack of regard, or even special treatment. But keeping an already-invisible illness a secret compounds the situation, limiting social contacts and preventing needed support.

The disconnected observer would judge you to be healthy and have expectations for you as a healthy functioning person. Being judged or even perceiving such judgment creates an additional stress upon both the patient and loved ones. "If only those who see me looking so healthy could experience my tinnitus for a day, I think they would not be so quick to judge," said a friend, whose ringing in her ears has persisted for several years. Those with recurring migraine headaches and back pain would most likely concur with her.

I once supervised an employee whose work ranged from brilliant to nonexistent, due to her invisible illness. I was ready to fire her by the time she finally told me the details of her experience with chronic illness. We were both culpable in that situation. I could have

> Being judged or even perceiving such judgment creates an additional stress upon both the patient and loved ones.

asked more questions. I could have created a safer space for her to confide in me. I did not do all that I could have to help her. She also could have helped me by sharing health information that would have led to the understanding and validation she needed.

Perhaps the story Paul Donoghue tells in his book *Sick and Tired of Feeling Sick and Tired: Living with Invisible Chronic Illness*, written with Mary Siegel, may be helpful. He describes the different ways two people were treated at a passport agency. A woman standing in line was experiencing such excruciating pain from her fibromyalgia that she longed to tell someone so she could move to the head of the line. Then a man in a wheelchair entered the room. He was immediately attended to by a passport agent, who brought him everything he needed, helped him complete and sign the paperwork, and sent him on his way. The woman was devastated, knowing she'd be in line and in pain for a longer time. A wheelchair is recognizable; her pain was not evident to anyone but herself. Following this story, Donoghue says, "[The woman's] experience at the passport agency typifies the stressful consequences of chronic invisible illnesses. The quality of this pain is so different from transient aches and pains that language is inadequate to the task of describing it."[1]

While the illness itself and the resulting pain may be the hardest to handle, invisibility remains emotionally taxing when friends and family are unable to acknowledge the condition. My mother had few complaints about her life with my father, but she was troubled by the judgments of others who had no clue about the exhaustion she experienced in caring for him. Neither one of them appeared to be ill, and Dad's diabetes was kept under wraps, so support and encouragement were not forthcoming and they continued to struggle alone. Both of my parents enjoyed being with friends, and Dad was especially social. Perhaps if Dad had confided in friends, they might have helped him rather than walk away in frustration from outbursts that came from low blood sugar. I know Mother would have enjoyed dinner parties more if she wasn't concerned with keeping a watchful eye on Dad's behavior.

A fellow church member with multiple sclerosis had sung in the choir, assisted with quilting, and taught Sunday school for many years. It was relatively easy for her to continue that schedule in the early years of her diagnosis. As these tasks became increasingly difficult, in part due to symptoms and effects unseen by others, she resigned from teaching and dropped out of the quilting group. She became apologetic to those who complained about her withdrawal and developed a sense of unworthiness she had never experienced before. Talking with a pastor who was present with her, listened to her, and sought to understand the difficulty she was having enabled her to tell a small group of friends. They, in turn, cleared a path for her to be as involved as she was able to be without placing unrealistic expectations or judgments on her. Sometimes, along this journey, there really are great moments of win–win.

Invisibility can lead to unnecessary testing and questioning, as well as ongoing insurance issues. You may feel frustrated and out of control and decide to give up. Don't! Seeking support from a counselor or spiritual advisor may give you the confidence you need to continue to find answers for your or your loved one's condition.

What Could Help?

You need to decide if you wish to keep your invisible condition private or if you want to involve those around you. This chapter concludes with stories of how these ideas helped others.

- Talk with someone in similar circumstances, see a counselor, or seek support from a clergyperson.
- Find a way to educate and inform others so we do not always feel negatively judged for ebbing interest and participation in daily activities. Suggest a book, movie, article, or pass along a Facebook post that provides the information we want others to know.
- Find people in our faith community or friendship circles who become educated about our condition and then provide support, assistance, understanding, and encouragement as needed.
- Know that our situation is never invisible to Jesus. (See Matt 19:1–10.)

It took nearly eleven years before Linda was diagnosed with Lyme disease. Not only did the physicians struggle with her myriad of symptoms, her family questioned her and encouraged her to "think healthy thoughts." Because she was so ill and unable to attend to her many responsibilities as a parent and spouse, Linda remains both surprised and relieved today that her husband stayed with her and she has good relationships with her children. Also difficult for Linda was the nagging feeling that maybe she didn't have an illness at all, that her symptoms were psychological and there was no medical cause or care. Whenever she had a good day, nearly symptom free, she felt guilty, as if her complaints were fraudulent. If you are in a similar situation, I hope Linda's story will encourage you to keep looking for answers.

Jesus Sees You

You or your loved ones may want to seek out some of the reminders in the Bible that show us how we are never invisible to Jesus. The story of Zacchaeus tells us he was up in a tree because he wanted to see Jesus but was too short. He may also have been hiding from the crowd, because he was a notorious tax collector. The most important part of this story to you may be how Jesus stopped at the base of the tree and called up to Zacchaeus. The tax collector may have been hidden in the branches and not easy to see, but Jesus saw him, loved him, pronounced him redeemed, and had dinner with him.

There are multiple examples of Jesus seeing what others might not. From Matthew 8:14: "When Jesus entered Peter's house, he saw his mother-in-law lying in bed with a fever." In the story of Jesus feeding the five thousand (Mark 6), the disciples saw a crowd they thought needed to go home and leave them alone. Jesus saw and responded to their need for food. Jesus wept as he saw his friend Mary grieving at the death of her brother. "When Jesus saw her weeping, and the Jews who came with her also weeping, he was greatly disturbed in spirit and deeply moved. He said, 'Where have you laid him?' They said to him, 'Lord, come and see.' Jesus began to weep" (John 11:33–35).

The pain, the illness, the condition may be without visible symptoms. People uncomfortable with illness may not acknowledge the struggle of those who are ill. But we can always count on Jesus to see us, to weep with us, and to respond in love, even when we feel invisible.

Dealing with ongoing treatment and all that may entail, maintaining interpersonal relationships, and managing the invisibility of the condition are three of the main challenges you and your family face as you adjust to your life after the diagnosis. While not insurmountable, they each cause stress and need resolution to continue to move forward into a new life of hope and joy.

For Reflection and Discussion

1 What strategies have you developed to overcome or incorporate treatment issues into your life?

2 Have you or could you talk with a close friend about your or a loved one's invisible illness as a step toward educating others about how they may be able to help you or your family?

3 Which of the stories in this chapter describe issues you could relate to? How are they helpful?

4 What have you learned through the challenges you face that might have positive impact on future difficulties?

4

What If the Patient Is My Child?

CARMEN'S DAUGHTER, Anita, was born with spina bifida, a birth defect in which part of the embryonic structure that develops in the baby's brain and spinal cord fails to close or develop. Spina bifida occurs in various degrees of severity. Born with the most severe form, Anita's spinal cord and membranes were exposed. Soon after birth, she had a surgical procedure to place the spinal cord and exposed tissue inside her body, covering them with muscle and skin. While the surgery reduced her vulnerability to infection, the lower half of her body was paralyzed.

Carmen thought she was at fault for her daughter's condition, because spina bifida results from a combination of genetic and environmental risk factors. A single mom, she was too busy caring for her baby to dwell on her own guilt, and took immediate steps to ensure as normal a life as possible for her daughter. Carmen was raised on a cattle-and-crop farm and is familiar with both hard work and setbacks. Her husband divorced her shortly after her daughter's birth, citing his inability to raise a child with a defect as his reason for abandoning his family. Before her daughter was two years old, Carmen was living with her parents in order to afford and provide the care Anita required.

Because Anita's cognitive abilities were not affected and the local school system was able to make accommodations for her, Carmen enrolled her in kindergarten when she was five years old. Carmen was able to return to work, move into her own home, and be available as Anita needed her throughout her childhood and adolescence. Often overwhelmed by the hours of care Anita required, Carmen reached out to other parents of chronically ill children for support.

When she felt the darkness of depression descending, she reached for her Bible, trusting God's words of presence and comfort to sustain her. Both she and Anita have received therapy to overcome emotional issues resulting from her daughter's condition. Carmen summarized their life together:

> It was really awful in the beginning. I was scared and felt like it was my fault, but my parents took us in and encouraged me as they always had. My life was more than hoisting Anita into our car and stashing her wheelchair in the trunk until we arrived at our destination when I reversed the effort. I had a career, friends, and my church. Anita went to school, had disagreements with friends, and went to homecoming and prom; all with extra accommodations to make it possible. We never wasted any time on "if only." Our life is good.

Anita is now a college graduate and is employed full-time in a community several states away from her mother. Anita remains mobile through her chair and a hand device on her van's steering wheel to control acceleration and braking as she drives. Although Carmen described her experience as a single mom of a chronically ill child in positive terms, she did talk at length about her personal adjustments and the concerns she continued to have as Anita grew up. "I had my parents nearby and that made all the difference in the world. I don't know what it would have been like, if I had been totally alone."

Obtaining information about single parents raising children who are ill is difficult. The most recent study I found is from 2007 and highlights the fact that there has been little study on this subject. The TIDES International Depression/Anxiety Epidemiological Study indicates the impact on mothers to be more severe than on fathers. Dr. Heather Quittner, principal investigator, says, "Mothers often don't get enough support from their spouse and they end up handling the load." I took a leap from their results to suggest how challenging it must be for single parents. The need for counseling and emotional support may be greater for mothers, whether they have a partner or not. The TIDES study also "found that more than 55 percent of the children's primary caregivers were anxious. These parents feel isolated and stressed by such challenges as obtaining insurance when a child has a pre-existing condition and the financial strain of co-payments for doctors' visits and medications."[1]

The difficulty of coping with chronic and serious illness increases exponentially when the patient is a child. No parent ever wants to see their child suffer. In the minds of most parents, for a child to be seriously or chronically ill is not the natural order of things. I was a very young mom when my oldest child was ill for the first time at

Ten Ways to Cope with a Child's Chronic Illness

Although the issues raised throughout this book may resonate with you as the parent of a chronically ill child, the following ideas are provided just for you.

1. Educate yourself and your child.

2. Get professional and community support.

3. Create and follow an action for treatment and care.

4. Communicate openly, honestly, and directly with your child and medical practitioners.

5. Do not be afraid to be your child's advocate.

6. Manage the elements of your life you can control and help your child assume self-management as they are able.

7. Remember to be a parent.

8. In addition to providing fun for your child, seek enjoyment for yourself too.

9. Adapt to your circumstances positively so you are able to grow.

10. Your adaptations and coping abilities are seen and repeated by your children. As you grow, your chronically ill child will too.[2]

age seven. I think I was too young to worry about the effects of a ruptured appendix, and I never questioned the private room or the constant flow of antibiotics to prevent further spread of the bacterial infection coursing through his bloodstream. I didn't know how close he came to dying. I'm certain my experience led to me becoming a hyper-vigilant parent by the time my second child was born.

This is one of the few times in this book when I need to say I can only use my imagination to try to understand what it feels like to be the parent of a child with a condition that is not only chronic but potentially life threatening. I did, however, have the assistance of my precious friend Beth, who lived and survived her experience.

Serious Illness

Beth's son Brian was almost nine years old, a third-grader with lots of friends. His younger brother was three years old. Beth said,

> Suddenly, Brian began wetting his pants at school, and over the next few weeks it happened more often. Then one night after dinner Brian sat at the table doing homework. I heard a strange, low guttural sound and saw that it came from him, his face contorted in a way I had never seen before. Immediately afterward he lost bladder control. I felt queasiness in my abdomen that quickly spread throughout my body like wildfire, a foreboding of difficulties to come. I rushed to comfort him, telling him I'd call the doctor in the morning; we'd figure out what was happening; it wasn't his fault.

Everyone had a troubled night. Beth told me about her memory of the appointment with the neurologist as though it had just happened. She described the seizure Brian had in front of the doctor and how an MRI was scheduled immediately. "It was a frontal lobe brain tumor," she said. "The seizures would get progressively worse as the tumor grew larger, so surgery was necessary." The surgeon removed the central body and the surrounding cells of the tumor, but Brian needed radiation to kill any remaining cancer cells.

Beth took a three-month leave of absence from work and drove every weekday morning for seven weeks to radiation treatments at a hospital twenty-five miles away. She always took her younger son with them and sometimes treated the trips as a special family outing. She struggled to care for her three-year-old while Brian was receiving his treatments and worried about giving both boys the attention they required. "After the treatments were over, I made the decision to leave my job as my sons were my first priority," she said.

For the next five years, Beth enjoyed being with her sons, resuming regular family routines as much as possible. Beth told me that all that time in the car with both her boys drew them closer to her and to one another. Instead of shutting down emotionally as some seriously ill children do, Brian opened up, asking questions and talking about his feelings. Beth got to know both boys better and soon recognized Brian's outgoing nature and ability to talk with adults.

When Brian's follow-up checkup with the neurologist revealed no sign of the cancer, Beth made plans to return to work. "But one night, again watching him do his homework, I noticed him writing very slowly, deliberately, and unable to concentrate on his work. I immediately felt chills run down my spine and into my legs. Fearing the worst, I called the neurologist for an appointment." There was a new tumor, and it was located in an area of the brain that couldn't be entered without causing permanent damage.

A second surgery was scheduled. The surgeon removed as much as possible and did cause some damage to Brian's brain. The tumor was still there and Brian had lost some cognitive ability. Beth said deciding what to do next was agonizing. She said,

> Brian could have additional chemotherapy that may or may not be effective but would diminish his quality of life. Or we could take him home and provide hospice care. What a decision. If Brian only had up to six months of life, we wanted it to be quality. If he had the treatment, he would be hospitalized far from home and would be very ill, without the promise of recovery.

Too many parents face this painful decision without the spiritual support needed to make and live with their choice. During the days Beth and her husband were trying to decide what to do, her church offered a healing service for those with serious illnesses. "We felt called to attend as a family, not understanding how our presence would change anything."

Beth described a very moving and powerful worship service of love and hope, with singing that connected her to others in pain.

> For the first time since Brian's diagnosis I was able to move outside myself, and I connected with the people around me in loving ways. After several days of reflection, we decided not to proceed with chemotherapy. While it was the hardest decision I ever made, afterward I never looked back.

Today, Beth talks about the healing service as the point at which she knew how completely God loved her, "that I was a member of earth's family and not alone in my pain." The healing service changed the lives of Beth, her husband, and both of their sons. They never discussed what had occurred during the service, but her family felt the positive effects. Beth knew God's love was strong enough to hold her and her family, and they continued to love and even enjoy being with Brian in the last weeks of his life.

Like many whose loved ones are actively dying, Beth's family too was told to help him let go of his fears about leaving them behind. Beth said, "The nurse told us to stroke his skin and tell him it's okay to go, that we'll be okay, we love him and we always will." Beth described this intimate experience. "I felt as though God was in our midst as we helped Brian face the death of his physical body." She said it felt like God had wrapped their family in love, giving them the strength and energy they needed. She will always love and miss her son, and she is grateful that she has learned to listen to the silent words from God.

Extra Care Is Needed

As Beth's story shows, caring for a seriously or chronically ill child requires additional hours of childcare, the need to be available at a moment's notice, and emotional strength. According to a study published in the *Journal of Child Health Care*, "Parents of chronically ill children, mothers in particular, are disadvantaged in society probably due to the challenge of combining child care with work and leisure time."[3] Many parents of children with leukemia or other childhood cancers, for example, found they were unable to continue working outside the home. In two-parent families, the parent with the most earning power usually stayed on the job while the other provided the daily care. As Carmen shared, single parents have an additional burden, often without the wherewithal to ensure security while coping with the child's needs.

Seeking outside support, including counseling, may be necessary, whether the patient is a child or an adult, but appears to be more critical for the parent(s) of an ill child. Many communities offer support groups to parents of children with specific illnesses; one of those groups could be helpful to you. Wise parents do not try to live through this experience alone.

Siblings Are Affected Too

Jillian was a senior in high school and her brother, Jack, was just thirteen when his cancer was discovered during a routine physical for football. It was thyroid cancer, addressed immediately by surgery. "I saw him when he came out of surgery. It was terrible. He was vomiting and crying in pain, and he was holding my hand." The only thing Jillian knew about cancer was that her grandfather had died of it when she was ten years old. "Nobody talked about it," she said. "I only knew cancer was serious and people who got it died. I was afraid my brother was dying, but I couldn't say that to my parents."

> Seeking outside support, including counseling, may be necessary, whether the patient is a child or an adult, but appears to be more critical for the parent(s) of an ill child.

Jillian told me her parents were probably afraid too but didn't talk about her brother's illness with her—not surprising, since many families have trouble deciding what to share with children and what to keep private. She said she recalls just one focused conversation about Jack's surgery and expected recovery. "Both Mom and Dad remained positive and hopeful, so I believed that the surgery took care of everything. If Dad said Jack would be okay, I trusted that." There were, however, five additional operations and follow-up radiation treatments, resulting in his isolation for a time. "He was like the boy in a bubble," she said. When Jillian needed to talk about her fears, she discussed them with friends.

Close family friends, neighbors, and Jillian's best friend cared for her during the days and weeks her parents were away from home. Looking back on the ways her brother's illness affected her life, Jillian said she experienced light moments too. She told me hilarious stories about playing the "my brother has cancer card." She said she was worried and she cared about her brother, but she also realized his illness could give her a pass when she didn't feel like completing her homework, getting out of bed, or meeting other responsibilities of a seventeen-year-old. Always reliable, dependable, and mature for her age, she never did anything unsafe or illegal, but, she says, "I had a license for drama, and I used it."

Her brother, in remission for more than fifteen years, remains on the medication protocol he began after his treatments. For the rest of Jack's life, his physician will monitor the activity of Jack's thyroid. Each year, for four to six weeks, he goes off his medication and is rechecked for any changes. This annual process continues to affirm his remission, but every year during the time he is off his medication, his body responds as if he has no thyroid at all. He is groggy and grumpy, and gains weight.

Despite these effects, Jack follows the regimen religiously. Soon after his initial surgery, he was back on the football field and played throughout high school and into college. His first professional position was teaching high school physical education. Health and wellness are his focus, with a special interest in helping young people who are unable to participate in sports due to a disability. For example, Jack has worked individually with children who have mobility issues, engaging them in swimming as sport.

Siblings of a chronically ill child may experience a greater bewilderment than the parents, who typically receive detailed information about their child's condition and treatment. Kara's brother Ethan's leukemia was also discovered through school sports. He was weak and tired during practice, so his coach recommended he see a physician. Everyone in the family was startled and alarmed at his diagnosis. Kara understood what was happening, and her parents were forthcoming about the days ahead. They were concerned about Ethan's prognosis but were also aware of the strides that have been made in treating childhood leukemia. Practical, steady, and down to earth, they made the necessary arrangements for treatment and ensured his ongoing care. They handled setbacks and emergencies with grace and provided information to the rest of the family to prevent needless worry. They took precautions when Ethan's immune system was compromised and gave him the freedom to be a teenager whenever they could. Kara was able to care about her brother and be involved in his care, and enjoyed her high-school years as well.

A life-threatening crisis occurred several years into remission when Ethan was diagnosed with an additional cancer. Without a successful bone marrow transplant, he would die. His younger sister, Kara, rose to the occasion. Together, she and Ethan underwent the testing and counseling required prior to the surgeries. Although Kara was young and had never had an operation before, she was determined to make this contribution to her brother's life. Brother and sister had always been close, and the transplant deepened their bond. Ethan recovered well, but his bones will always be fragile as a result of the chemotherapy. He remains in remission, and both he and Kara have moved on with their close, but independent lives.

> Siblings of a chronically ill child may experience a greater bewilderment than the parents, who typically receive detailed information about their child's condition and treatment.

Who Takes Responsibility?

Deciding when to allow the child to take responsibility for treatment and follow-up care needs to be based primarily on the severity of results if the child fails to treat the disease correctly. Many physicians agree that the best mistake would be for parents to exercise too much control rather than too little.

Ethan and Kara's parents had never been the controlling kind, but Ethan's illness did raise the question of how to find a balance between letting him be responsible for himself and protecting him from further complications. This is an issue many parents of chronically ill children have. Randy's daughter, Zoe, has type 1 diabetes. As Zoe ages, she has wanted more control over her life, and Randy and his wife have let go slowly. It is important to them to monitor her behavior and keep her safe while allowing their daughter the freedom to make her own decisions. Occasionally, Zoe's food choices compromise her body's ability to regulate the insulin she takes daily, but a trip to the hospital gets her back on the right path. "She is learning," Randy said. "We just need to make sure she doesn't get into serious trouble." Ethan's parents never had to address teenage rebellion, but Zoe's parents might. It is difficult to know what behavior is due to adolescent angst or rebellion and what is a symptom of the health condition.

Elizabeth Leis-Newman, senior editor at McKnight's Long-Term Care News, cites comments made by the investigators in a 2006 study on caring for chronically ill children, suggesting that parents think about turning over illness management to their child similarly to the way they think about that child learning to drive. "There needs to be a learner's permit. At some point, you let go, but there needs to be a bridge to the child managing his or her own treatment." Leis-Newman says, "We work with parents on that so by the time the child is 17 or 18, they can relinquish control."[4]

Discerning parents give up control incrementally. If a child can be responsible for taking medication as required while at home, it may be time to allow them to take it away from home as well. Together, parents and the child can make these decisions, although a physician's guidance may be helpful. The article cited above also said that when teens were asked about what would motivate them to be more compliant when managing their illness, the researchers were surprised to find that a special outing with Mom or Dad as a reward would be helpful.

Are There Advantages to an Early Diagnosis?

This is not merely a positive spin on a tough diagnosis. Researchers continue to study the effects of early diagnosis on the way a condition advances. Some of the questions being asked include:

- Is it due to physiology or the developmental emotional state?
- Does youth make it easier to move forward?
- Does the adolescent notion of invincibility add years to the life of someone with a progressive disease?

As painful as it was for Jennifer to hear when she was still a teenager that she had a chronic illness, she is quick to talk about the advantages of being young. When her rheumatoid arthritis was discovered, Jennifer was still young and healthy enough to begin a treatment regimen that continues to help her avoid some of the typical complications of the disease. She thought she would have had several surgeries by now, but they have not been necessary. As for the nursing-home life she feared, more than twenty years after her diagnosis, she cares for herself, her children, her home, and her expansive yard.

Two celebrity situations also indicate the earlier you recognize an illness and start treatment, the better your prospects are for a longer-than-expected lifespan. Regarded as one of the most brilliant theoretical physicists since Einstein, Stephen Hawking was diagnosed in 1963 with motor neuron disease (amyotrophic lateral sclerosis or ALS). The stories about Stephen Hawking's atypically long life with ALS suggest that his young age at diagnosis and

Discerning parents give up control incrementally.

beginning treatment as early as he did have prolonged his life. Like Jennifer, he has had fewer complications that occur in patients much older than him.

Michael J. Fox has Parkinson's disease. Also diagnosed young, at age twenty-nine, he continues his acting career, although he fights to get out the right words and sometimes struggles to keep his jerky movements from controlling a scene. He had planned to survive long enough to help find a cure, but even he is surprised to find himself where he is today. An article in *AARP* magazine tells a delightful story of Michael trying to bring a cup of coffee to his wife, Tracy. He barely got it poured and then slopped all over the place carrying it to her. By the time he handed it to her, saying, "Here's your coffee, dear, enjoy," there was little remaining in the cup. And they laughed! Their passion for life, together with their children, helps them move forward. When talking about all the barriers they face due to Michael's illness, Tracy says to him, "Hold my hand and we'll get over that." His age at diagnosis is given as the reason for his longevity, but the way he and his family have accepted and moved forward with their lives must receive some credit.

We seldom view celebrities as regular people, just like us, but the stories of Fox and Hawking may provide not only inspiration—as the Hawking article gave my husband—but also the awareness that no one is immune from the challenges of living. The popular movie about Hawking's life with ALS, *The Theory of Everything*, presents facts about the disease and shows both his struggles and his tenacity in meeting the demands of his condition. The books and articles published by and about him are often helpful to others with ALS and other pain and illness. Being able to watch Michael J. Fox in his role as an attorney on the television drama *The Good Wife* and read articles depicting his family life gives courage and inspiration to those living with similar conditions, albeit very different financial situations.

Hawking and Fox have experienced better outcomes than those diagnosed with the same conditions later in life. I share their stories because you may find inspiration and hope in them. I realize, however, the message may or may not carry over to other illnesses. Still, the hope offered by early diagnosis lies in the opportunities afforded by ongoing research and advances in treatment.

My dad was diagnosed with type 1 diabetes in 1928, decades before self-administered glucose tests and insulin pumps were available. Age notwithstanding, diabetics with renal failure today routinely receive not only a new kidney but also a new pancreas, in effect "curing" their disease. In 1996, when David had his liver transplant, the doctor said the longest living survivor had added eleven years to his life. The year David died, 2006, the projection had risen to eighteen years; today, surgeons predict that a successful liver transplant can increase life expectancy by as much as twenty-two years.

Whenever the diagnosis of a serious or chronic condition in a child occurs, life changes forever. Many of the people I talked with are people of faith, yet several not only questioned God's wisdom in their child's illness but became and remained angry for a long time. Trying to reconcile human ideas about life "as it should be" with God's love and compassion can be difficult—too hard to do alone. Support from a counselor or group helped many of them through periods of anger and loneliness. Even when feeling too angry to turn to God for help, it may be helpful to rely on the prayers of family, friends, and fellow church members. Others want to help, and standing in the gap during this difficult time is one way they can provide support.

Your experience with an ill child may be very different from any situations I've described, but it is my earnest prayer that you have found something in this chapter to make your life a little easier. More than anything, I pray that God's loving presence will hold you secure and give you the strength and courage you need every day.

Trying to reconcile human ideas about life "as it should be" with God's love and compassion can be difficult—too hard to do alone.

For Reflection and Discussion

1 In what ways does the diagnosis of a child's condition alter your life?

2 How have you managed caring for yourself and the rest of your family while dealing with the needs of your child who is ill?

3 What additional information or supports might improve your situation? Where and how might you find what you need?

4 How has assurance of God's presence with you in your difficulty contributed to your quality of life?

5
What Can I Control?

THE DIAGNOSIS was out of our control. The treatment plan was out of our control. The side effects and results of treatment were out of our control. David and I felt like there was nothing we could control, and we did not like that.

Whether faced with a chronic or serious health condition or not, there is little in life that any of us can control. In fact, it is the illusion of control that frustrates us when we are unable to do anything about our circumstances. Despite our longings to be in charge, there will always be situations, behaviors, even thoughts and feelings that remain out of our control.

The fear and loss I experienced when feeling so out of control were tempered by two things. First, I finally understood why my mother had arranged and manipulated things in my dad's life. I think controlling potentially dangerous situations helped her live with Dad's illness. Her example led David and me to talk about what we could control. Knowing what we were in charge of lessened the fear and helped us see opportunities rather than losses. Second and most important, while I believe that we never entirely give up the illusion of control, I was able to let go long enough to hear what God was saying about human limitations. I found these notes in my journal from 1995, when David had his first medical emergency: I wrote, "Praise be to the Lord, to God our Savior, who daily bears our burdens" (Ps 68:19). And I copied from my daily calendar, "When your trial comes, put it into the will of God and climb into that

> It is the illusion of control that frustrates us when we are unable to do anything about our circumstances.

will as a little child climbs into its mother's arms," by Hannah Whitall Smith.

Closing the journal, on a particularly fear-filled day, my eyes went to the cover décor that held the first verse of the Serenity Prayer. Through my tears, I gave thanks for such a sense of God's nearness. Since that time, my journals haven't always been filled with gratitude, but the loving reminders of God I wrote about often helped me and my family through many challenging times.

When living with a chronic illness or pain, it makes sense to use our energy for those things we can control. I remember watching my friend Barb fold laundry at a time when her life was turned upside down by a crisis. When I asked her about her commitment to properly folded towels, she replied, "It feels normal." When so much was out of her control, Barb reached for something familiar. Her guiding verses through months of suffering were these: "Set

Praise be to the Lord, to God our Savior, who daily bears our burdens.

Serenity Prayer

God grant me the serenity
to accept the things I cannot change;
courage to change the things I can;
and wisdom to know the difference.
Living one day at a time;
enjoying one moment at a time;
accepting hardships as the pathway to peace;
taking, as He did, this sinful world
as it is, not as I would have it;
trusting that He will make all things right
if I surrender to His Will;
that I may be reasonably happy in this life
and supremely happy with Him
forever in the next.
Amen.[1]

—Reinhold Niebuhr (1892–1971)

your minds on things that are above, not on things that are on earth, for you have died, and your life is hidden with Christ in God" (Colossians 3:2–3). Eventually, she was ready to take steps into the future, focusing on what she could control and accepting what was beyond her human limitations.

Radical Acceptance

Sue knew the only true way out of her depression, and through her grief, was to accept Jon's condition. She was confused and troubled by others who loved him and insisted on holding out hope that Jon would have a miraculous healing, restoring him to his former self. "They are convinced that if we pray hard enough and refuse to accept his condition, God would cure Jon of all that disabled him," Sue told me. "That is what gives them hope, but it complicated the situation for me." She said,

> Holding on to hope led us to false expectations about the progress he could make. It just put me in a very dark place. I took the word hope out of my vocabulary for a time, and worked on radical acceptance of Jon as he is today, disability and all. We could come to terms with it, we could deal with it, and we could adapt to it. That doesn't mean it is easy. At times, it is excruciatingly difficult. But we push on and find out what works for us and what doesn't.

After arriving at what she labeled radical acceptance, Sue was able to add hope back into her life with a fuller meaning than she'd originally held. One of the blogs Sue followed regularly was written by a young woman whose husband has ALS. The writer of the blog posted several columns sharing her family's story of trying to hold on to hope that the diagnosis was wrong. They prayed for a miracle and were stunned when their prayers were not answered as they wanted. "Over time, however," Sue said, "the writer began describing the signs of spiritual and emotional healing that occurred in her family. It seems like they did experience a miracle." Sue told me how she grew along with that family, allowing her to put miraculous recovery into perspective and open her eyes to God's daily activity in their lives. She said, "Maybe we should reframe what we mean by a miracle. Rather than waiting for the big and showy biblical event, we need to be on the lookout for the less dramatic but still miraculous events we experience every day." A comment by a chaplain was also helpful to Sue: "I used to think a miracle was when a patient would get cured of their disease, but I think the true miracle is being able to live with the illness they have." Reading about and talking with others whose lives had also changed dramatically led Sue to claim acceptance, the reality of miracles and ongoing hope. "My growth experience wouldn't be as strong without having all three of those in my mindset."

Acceptance is seldom complete and never final, even when we think we've done all we can. Each new symptom or turn of events can catch us reverting to denial or anger, but ongoing acceptance of the condition is important for healing and the ability to live with hope. The best we can do most of the time is to accept where we are now, recognizing that we will have more to accept in the future. Acceptance comes step-by-step, piece-by-piece, incident-by-incident.

In my family of origin, we had multiple experiences with acceptance. One of my mother's favorite Bible passages, Philippians 4:11–12, reflected her desire to rely on God's promise and presence throughout her life with Dad: "Not that I am referring to being in need; for I have learned to be content with whatever I have. I know what it is to have little, and I know what it is to have plenty." Both of my parents trusted God's presence in their lives, and Mother found ways to be content with her unpredictable life. Because she knew God was with her, Mother found contentment even during hospitalizations and Dad's long hours connected to a dialysis machine.

My father, however, described himself as a realist. When he was diagnosed with kidney failure as a result of childhood diabetes, he needed to participate in grief counseling with the hospital social worker before he could be considered for dialysis. He refused to see

> Acceptance is seldom complete and never final, even when we think we've done all we can.

her after his third visit when she invited him to share his goals for the next five years. "My goals for the next five years?" he barked. "In five years, I expect to be six feet under." Not eligible for a transplant at that time because of maximum age restrictions, dialysis would keep him alive for a time, and he was furious that she would ask "such a stupid question." Giving up or giving in to the illness is not the same as acceptance and seldom leads to hope. Mother tried to ease the relationship with the social worker and did her best to control the new situation in which my parents found themselves. My father died less than three years after his conversation with the social worker. His early death was painful but not surprising to me.

My husband accepted his condition fairly quickly and refused to give up. David recovered with remarkable speed from his liver transplant, and for the first several months following his release from the hospital, our life together felt like it had prior to his illness. Well, almost. He was taking a combination of pills that exceeded what he had feared initially, and he had to organize medications and schedules to ensure they were taken as directed, before or after meals, first thing in the morning, last thing before bed. Also new to our routine was a weekly trip to the local clinic for blood work, followed by a report on the results and consultation with his transplant coordinator. But he was able to go back to work, our family life began to settle into a routine, and there were few surprises. At last we knew what needed to be done and we were able to do it.

Some articles, blog posts, and advice from helpful friends suggest that arriving at acceptance is a step-by-step, incremental process. It may be incremental, but the path is more spiral-like than a straight line or progression through a recommended ten-step plan. Sue's journey to acceptance required her to give up false hopes of dramatic improvements and face the reality of each moment. Jon's condition may continue to improve, but her family lives with each day and each experience as it arrives. They are doing their best to live with the truth, the reality of limitations, knowing things can change and moving forward through the changes.

Moving On

While in the throes of emergencies and the immediate needs of the patient, it is easy enough to stop participating in the outside world. However, eventually someone will ask, "What's for supper?" The time comes when the children say, "Don't I need to go to school?" Despite any initial and foggy beliefs to the contrary, life continues to move forward after diagnosis, for the patient and the caregiver, and especially for those outside the situation who may have expectations for you.

The rest of the family, and those outside the family, begin to press for your involvement with them. Assistance from others begins to dwindle, and requests for your participation increase. Both the patient and family members need to establish new routines. It took my management team at work saying, "How much longer are we covering for you without getting any direction?" for me to acknowledge that life and responsibilities continue. It was time for us to figure out what we needed to do to continue to care for ourselves and honor our commitments to others. Although the crisis state may last much longer than anticipated, the time comes when we begin to get back in touch with all aspects of life.

You may wonder just how to do that when life has changed so dramatically. David was able to return to work part-time after treatment of his acute condition began, but Jon, Sue's husband, may never be employed again. Following his brainstem stroke at age forty-five, all of his family's energy went into keeping him alive and getting him through rehabilitation. Sue recalls, "God took care of us through meals from church, childcare by neighbors, and so much support from friends. We weren't worried about money. We just wanted Jon to recover." Jon had been a community police officer, with excellent fringe benefits and sick leave. Most of his expenses were covered by his medical insurance. Jon's benefits, however, finally ran out, and Sue's family agreed she needed to provide financially for the family and maintain appropriate medical insurance. This was not an easy transition. The children had to

> Although the crisis state may last much longer than anticipated, the time comes when we begin to get back in touch with all aspects of life.

assume greater responsibility for themselves and to contribute to household maintenance while continuing to be full-time students.

If the person with the illness has been the primary economic provider for your family, you may want to apply for Social Security Disability Insurance. It can be hard to get through this process, whether completed by the ill person or the caregiver. Be aware that it will take longer if the illness has no outward symptoms and the diagnosis is incomplete. Completing the application, when financial help is most desperately needed, can be another major challenge. Obtaining help through the process from someone who knows the situation and cares can lessen the burden and move the application forward. The work ethic many of us were raised with and continue to be exposed to makes it hard to reach out for help, especially when seeking government assistance. Financial support exists for situations of need.

Sometimes creating the initial routine after diagnosis or emergency goes smoothly and life continues as expected. You want to know what to anticipate so you are not caught totally off guard if or when it happens. You manage your own care. You might depend on a family member, housemate, or caregiver to follow through with ongoing care. Whatever your situation, someone needs to take on the responsibility for continued attention to healthcare.

After my husband's first hospitalization, he was eager to assume full responsibility for his health as soon as he was well enough to do so. He picked up his prescriptions; he organized his medication cabinet and schedule, made his lab appointments and the phone calls that followed. After his transplant, he monitored his daily temperature, blood pressure, and blood counts. Watching for signs of rejection, he reported to his transplant coordinator regularly. We knew an infection could hit him hard, so we always reported any sustained spike in temperature.

David recovered from his transplant surgery quickly and did not experience any of the problems he was told to expect in the first weeks and months. We began thinking we could go back to the life we had and even took a brief trip out of state. Then, suddenly, he was hospitalized with an infection caused by the failure of auxiliary blood vessels to compensate for the arteries that were still healing. Infection followed infection, taking over our lives for nearly six months. We spent virtually every holiday from Thanksgiving through Lent in the hospital. Just before Easter, David was released from the hospital with a port so he could take antibiotics at home. That was his last dose of antibiotics and the end of the infections for several years.

We made only two more emergency room runs over the next ten years. The first was a midnight dash in Louisville, Kentucky, where we waited hours before he was finally diagnosed with a sinus infection and placed in a room that seemed like a luxury hotel suite. The second was an easy and relaxed drive to the local hospital for antibiotics and the good news that he just had the flu that was going around. In response to that hospitalization, he took greater care to avoid people who were ill. With the exception of the infections, his condition was stable for many years, and we were able to make the necessary accommodations.

Life from Death

We had two remarkable experiences following David's recovery from the series of infections. The first was receiving a letter from the family of David's donor, asking if we could meet. Organ recipients are allowed to write thank-you letters and send them to the hospital, and the letters are sent to the donor family only if they agree. David included our address in his letter, and was overwhelmed with emotion when he received a reply. We did have a bittersweet and treasured meeting with the family to share our sympathy and express our unending gratitude. The other experience happened at church. Large tree branches, shaped into crosses, were placed in the area for the forty days of Lent. On Easter Sunday, one of the crosses, now sprouting new life, had been placed at the entrance. A sign was placed on the cross, "Here is life out of death." It was a remarkable experience watching David's tears fall as we gave thanks not just for his new life but for the resurrection we were celebrating that Easter morning, for the life that mattered more to us than any other. God was with us, indeed.

With progressive illnesses like Parkinson's disease and rheumatoid arthritis, changes in the condition may move slowly, with time for patient and loved ones to gradually adjust. In some situations, another crisis precipitates the adjustment.

When Dianne's husband was first diagnosed with Parkinson's, they made the necessary adaptations and found enjoyment and support among their many friends. They were also able to keep up their busy travel schedule for many years. His disease progressed slowly. As his legs grew weaker, he fell repeatedly and had no choice but to use an adapted walker. More than thirteen years later, they can no longer go out as a couple or even entertain friends at home. Dianne needs support now, as she becomes the primary caretaker not only of Ron but also of their home. "I wish we would have downsized years ago, but we didn't, and I had to replace the furnace and the roof this winter. Ron deserves a comfortable home as long as he can still move around with the aid of his walker." Dianne knows she will not be able to care for Ron much longer in their home, so she spends as much time with him as possible. While he has therapy, she goes for a walk or workout, and sees her friends if there is time. Sometimes the way forward is prescribed by the health condition.

Beth's family lived normally for five years, but when Brian developed a new tumor, everything changed drastically and dramatically once again. The second time was a greater challenge as they soon realized he would not survive his condition. Rather than making preparations for family life to continue, Beth devoted herself to helping her son die in peace. Many days, the best thing she could do for him was to sit quietly at his side, holding his hand and telling him how special he was. On his more alert days, they talked, not about his illness or death, but about the fun things he'd enjoyed doing and some of his family memories. Each conversation with Brian was heart-wrenching for Beth, but she discovered she was stronger than she thought. She credits her unwavering faith in God's ability to bring good out of tragedy for her strength. She also depended on her priest and local parish for guidance, support, and ongoing care for herself.

If you are in a situation like Beth's, please do not try to handle it without help. You may not feel like talking or involving anyone else in your grief, but you may have friends who listen well and know how to be with you. Pastoral care providers are trained to provide a ministry of presence, by listening rather than advising, and will allow you to release your emotions safely.

Jennifer did recover from her surgeries, her depression, and her divorce. Knowing she would most likely need additional surgery in the future did not stop her from taking steps to creating a new life with her children. "My surgeon told me I'd need another operation on my leg within five years. But it didn't happen and it may never be needed. I learned something reassuring about leaving the future in God's hands." Nine years later, Jennifer coaches her children in soccer, has a job she loves, and is as physically active as she can be. She knows both the compartment syndrome (described in chapter 2) and her rheumatoid arthritis will be with her forever, even as she walks into a future she believes is blessed, no matter what happens next.

Moving on is not the same as denying the illness, leaving it behind you, or, as some suggest, "getting over it." Taking steps into the future is not to deny what has happened or may occur, but it is an important step to regaining even limited control of our lives. This is a critical time to remember and cling to God's faithfulness. As circumstances continue to change, you may feel stuck and immobilized by the illness. There may be days when it feels like the complications, grief, and effort involved in moving forward will never end, but we can seek to live according to Saint Paul's letter to the Romans: "No, in all these things, we are more than conquerors through him who loved us" (8:37). Allow the love and grace of God to accompany you. No matter what else has been upended, Paul continues, "For I am convinced that neither death, nor life, nor angels, nor rulers, nor things present, nor things to come, nor powers, nor height, nor depth, nor anything else in all creation, will be able to separate us from the love of God in Christ Jesus our Lord" (8:38–39).

> Taking steps into the future is not to deny what has happened or may occur, but it is an important step to regaining even limited control of our lives. This is a critical time to remember and cling to God's faithfulness.

Make a Plan

We found it helpful to create a plan, especially to prepare for emergencies or unusual events. Realistic planning gave us a sense of control over our response to David's illness. Planning for daily life, establishing new routines, and creating schedules for medication, treatments, and appointments helped restore order to our lives. Having a plan that fits the situation also allowed us to maintain relationships with others and support other family members as we all learned to live in a changed household.

After Sue recovered from depression and took time to work through her grief, she knew there was more work to do. Sue realized she needed to make two plans: one for self-care and the other for family life. Sue had to juggle her schedule to arrange time to see a counselor, get enough rest, and have some time for herself. She also took control of hiring and scheduling home healthcare providers. After some searching, she found someone skilled and interested enough to be with Jon consistently during her work hours. She asked Jon to take the lead in determining what kinds of outings they could resume and asked his advice as she planned new family activities. She even did some backup planning for those times when their original plans just wouldn't work.

Making a plan to deal with a long-term condition that may remain steady is different from planning for emergencies during acute phases. One family with a chronically ill child prepared a car kit, with a change of clothing, medications, medical documents, books, journal, and a deck of cards to be ready for any unexpected travel. The same family worked to maintain a reasonable housekeeping regimen and meal plan. They did not want to return from an emergency trip to dirty clothes, a messy house, and mold growing in their refrigerator. Of course, they tried to keep their car maintained and filled with gas. They weren't always fully prepared, but their efforts provided peace of mind.

Planning helps when your family begins to feel the illness has taken over your lives. Initially we struggled to see the outside world, much less deal with daily life. We weren't thinking about our jobs or family or any other responsibilities. Our focus was on the illness and a steady schedule of doctor visits. We were referred to a specialist to initiate the treatments that would resolve the immediate life-threatening issues. After receiving medication that would keep David out of danger during the treatment period, we recorded all the treatment dates for the next several months. Then, while we could not answer all our questions with any certainty, we did make preliminary decisions about employment, finances, and relationships outside our immediate family, and created a list of symptoms that required medical follow-up. We finally felt in control of something.

So . . . you have your plan, you seem to be moving along well, making adjustments, becoming more comfortable accepting the illness, and then . . . a deluge of grief. You can't identify where it originated. You thought you were through with those feelings of loss. You're even beginning to explore new activities and outlets and enjoying them. "Where did that come?" a woman asked. Many of us who are dealing with chronic illness or pain may carry around the deeply buried idea that this is just a temporary situation and good health is around the next corner. Predicting when those unconscious thoughts will conflict with reality is impossible. As heartbreaking as grief feels, those moments are part of the process of taking control of what you can and relying on God for the rest.

When You Are the Patient

This book was written for people living with the illness or pain and for their loved ones. This section is addressed directly to you. In order to give yourself the best care possible, you need to know that you are a precious human being, who has chronic pain or an illness. Your diagnosis does not define who you are. You are the same you on the inside even if your illness or condition has changed you physically. You remain the person you have been, beloved of God and equipped with gifts, interests, and dreams. A friend with

> Your diagnosis does not define who you are.

> For surely I know the plans I have for you, says the Lord, plans for your welfare and not for harm, to give you a future with hope.

> Your illness or condition is not caused by God for some greater purpose. However, you may find God drawing good from your situation.

HIV told me he thinks illness strips away all pretense and draws us back to who we really are. Beth, whose son died from his brain tumor, is now concerned with her own health issues as she ages. She maintains her interests and her passion for life, with a focus on learning. Beth believes each experience in life, good or bad, has something to teach us, and she values the opportunities she has to grow and to share her stories with others. Karen's experience with lung disease has led her to look for opportunities to learn and find good in her life, despite her changing condition. Perhaps you can find meaning for your life in Jeremiah 29:11: "For surely I know the plans I have for you, says the Lord, plans for your welfare and not for harm, to give you a future with hope."

If we define and identify ourselves by our work or what we do, the limits that come with unrelenting pain or illness may strip away our sense of meaning or self-worth. If Jon's self-image continues to be wrapped up in his work as a police officer, he would be hard-pressed to see himself as the same man he was before his stroke. Fortunately, he knew his role as husband and father came first, and his diminished cognitive capacity protects him from recalling all that he once was. He knows who he is now, still a husband, father, and child of God.

There may be ways to live out God's desire for your life that matches both your desire and your condition. I return to Karen's favorite Bible story and the very complicated path Joseph traveled to live out his dream. Another of my favorites is that beautiful line from the story of Esther, "Who knows? Perhaps you have come to royal dignity for just such a time as this" (Esther 4:14). To some, this is a story of fulfilling God's destiny. I understand "such a time as this" to be wherever you find yourself, knowing you are in God's caring presence. So, I repeat, your illness or condition is not caused by God for some greater purpose. However, like many of those whose stories I've told, you may find God drawing good from your situation.

Because your condition will impact how you continue to live, the following questions may be helpful in creating your own plan for the days ahead.

- How do you talk about your condition and to whom? When?
- How will you make arrangements for travel to treatments or therapy?
- What are the symptoms you must remain aware of?
- How can you anticipate emergencies and make preparations?

You may have questions and concerns related to employment, loss of income, or unforeseen expenses.

- Are there ways to modify your job duties or hours so you can continue to work?
- How might you develop other sources of income?
- If you're eligible for social security disability insurance or other income assistance, what do you need to do to apply?

You may have concerns about your living arrangements.

- Can your home accommodate your physical needs?
- Do you need to find another place to live or can your home be renovated to meet your new requirements?
- If you live alone, how can you continue to do that? What kinds of help and support will you need?

You may require prolonged periods of protective isolation and fear being lonely.

- How might you protect yourself, while still meeting your social needs?
- How could you connect with others when you are confined to your home or a single room?

You may feel too overwhelmed to even think of the questions, much less find answers for them. Just take charge of what you can and seek help when you need it.

Pastor Brian told me how his wife, Jane, planned for dealing with loneliness following some treatments. Whether the need for protective isolation is immediate or occurs intermittently, loneliness is likely. Jane is a faith-filled woman who trusts God for all things and needs personal relationships with friends and family. Six years into her remission from breast cancer, cancer was discovered in several additional places in her body. She needed to be isolated from others until the proper treatment could be identified and begin. She enjoyed telephone conversations, especially those aided by computer software (Skype and FaceTime) allowing her to see her visitors as they talked. Jane used both Facebook and CaringBridge[2] to stay in touch with friends and family. She kept a journal, detailing her life with God throughout her illness, and she often posted excerpts to which her friends could respond.

Creating a New Normal

Although the idea of a new normal is not a universal concept, what generally happens after the initial reactions begin to give way is that we find a different way to live. Living post-diagnosis has its challenges *and* can be very rewarding. You know now a cure is unlikely, but healing is possible. Healing is never ending and transformation is always a process. Some call this process of moving forward "rebuilding your life." Others seek a "new normal."

An Episcopal priest gave me some of the best advice I ever hated hearing: "Just put one foot in front of the other."

"But I don't want to, I just can't," I replied.

"You can and you will," he insisted.

He wasn't telling me to go out and get a new job, or to deep-clean my home, take flying lessons, or cure my husband. He was reminding me that I had a life, despite David's illness. I didn't know what to do, and moving my feet was the priest's idea to help me get started. I've already mentioned the starts and stops in my own

Take charge of what you can and seek help when you need it.

Healing is never ending and transformation is always a process.

process of acceptance, but our conversation strengthened my resolve to move on and trust God's mercy.

I had to get back to work. I had commitments that needed to be honored. Life was different from what it had been, but David was alive and our family could move forward. We just had to take those steps.

"New Normal" was used by economists following the financial crisis of 2007–2008, but Roger McNamee, founder of Elevation Partners, published his book *The New Normal* in 2004. There are also those who say "the new normal" was first used immediately following the events of September 11, 2001. But I found documentation of the phrase being used to the adjustments in life made after World War I. "In the years immediately after the end of World War I, a spate of books and articles addressed 'the new normal' that was expected to emerge after that conflict."[3] Wherever the expression originated, those I talked with personally about chronic/serious illness or pain used that expression to describe their life post-diagnosis.

The idea of creating a new normal helps us maintain hope and passion for living by focusing on what we can control. Settling into a new normal requires ongoing acceptance of changes and intentionally moving forward as you are able. David and I started

Is New Normal Real?

Some people who live with chronic illness claim a new normal does not exist or believe the phrase feeds into the lie that anything in life is normal. Yet, our expectations about our lives suggest that good health is one thing we consider to be normal. When our health is threatened, our traditional or typical ways of living are threatened. In order to survive and thrive, we need to have hope that we can work out a new normal.

using the phrase to describe our life change within two weeks of the diagnosis, but we had no idea how to normalize our life, and neither did our family, friends, or faith community. One day, soon after his diagnosis, David read an article about Stephen Hawking, who still spends his days in a wheelchair unable to care for himself, but is able to speak through a speech synthesizer. "Listen to this," David said, reading aloud. "Hawking says he always focused on what he could do and not what he could not do. If that made the difference for Hawking, that's good enough for me."

Reading that story inspired David's new motto for living: "If I encounter something I've never done and it is safe and I think I will enjoy it, I'm going to do it." He was creating and fulfilling his bucket list as he moved forward. David was a hoot after his transplant, seeking out new opportunities and often dragging me along with him. He was always on the lookout for experiences that were new, different, and entirely possible. We loved the challenges and life-enriching experiences in our "new normal." Just as life is not always about illness, doctors, and another new treatment, however, neither are our days always filled with exciting moments. Sometimes, daily life is just that. David cherished the gift of life he had received through his liver transplant. He became a fan of stopping to watch the birds or pick up litter on the ground, saying his illness gave him every chance to do just that. Noticing the opportunities he'd rushed past prior to his illness became an important part of David's new normal.

Taking some control, making decisions about how to survive and thrive in a new way, is life-giving. Knowing what we can and cannot control also keeps us mindful of God's work in our lives. Recognizing how hard it was to focus only on what I could control, I recalled the message I understood to be from God when David first got sick: "It will not be easy, but it will be all right." It took me a while to realize that I needed to value God's definition of "all right" and find the moments of grace. Most days that reminder kept us moving, even thriving, to the best of our ability.

> Taking some control, making decisions about how to survive and thrive in a new way, is life-giving. Knowing what we can and cannot control also keeps us mindful of God's work in our lives.

On their way to a new normal, Sue and Jon began making adaptations in their marriage and family life. She spoke of God's provision when she told me how her job working as a teaching assistant in a classroom with disabled children for the previous seven years had prepared her to help Jon. "I learned to do tube feedings, locate private areas in public spaces, and adapt activities to the child's abilities. How can I not thank God for that training and experience? Who knew I was being prepared to care for my own husband?" According to Sue, "Life goes on."

Jon's lack of depression and self-pity, plus a great sense of humor, contributed to Sue's plan to find a new normal. Without giving up and giving in, Sue realized that old expectations needed to be replaced. Jon would set the pace. Occasionally, she and the children followed through with previously made plans, but being able to involve Jon was a priority. When he felt well enough to walk, travel, or socialize, the family followed suit. Nothing would move as quickly as it had previously, and outings were limited to those that were accessible to him. They discovered, however, change has its positive impacts. They no longer take extended vacations, but they enjoy going for long drives. They enjoy regional events and special community celebrations in which they can participate at Jon's pace. Sometimes when going for a walk, Jon relies on his walker. At other times, he moves well, if slowly, without it. Sometimes alternative activities and locations are better suited for his condition and provide the desired experience. I remember being surprised by the number of state parks that are accessible to those unable to walk or walk too far. Sue and Jon have sought them out regularly.

Roger's adjustment to his amputation includes using a wheelchair until his prosthesis is ready and he is able to walk with it in place. Because his wife, Beth, is such a gentle caregiver, she would prefer Roger to move back into daily activity a little more slowly than he has. She was concerned a few weeks after his amputation when Roger fell getting out of the shower, moving from tub to chair. But the spill didn't slow him down. As long as a concert hall, a sports field, a restaurant, or a park has wheelchair access, Roger is ready to go. Beth stepped in as driver for the first months, but now she helps Roger get into their van and behind the wheel so they can continue to travel regionally. Road trips are part of their new normal as they discover the many opportunities for leisure and recreation without flying.

One of the benefits of technology is the access we can have to activities otherwise beyond our enjoyment. If migraines or eye pain prevents reading, most bestsellers can be listened to via digital downloads, library CD rentals, or through online services such as audible.com. You may want to Skype when you can't be out in public, stream relaxing music or meditations to work through pain, wear a device that automatically collects health data you need, or use Google to search for other technological advances that can provide what you are looking for as you re-create your lifestyle.

Whether you find the idea of creating a new normal useful, you are not without hope and not without opportunities to live in a new way. The condition is ongoing, but the daily experience may not always be bad. The symptoms may come and go, the severity of pain or incapacitation may be uneven and unpredictable, but you will experience good days as well as heartbreaking ones.

When Jennifer talked about her experiences in community theater as an adult with two chronic conditions, she said, "It was time to start living. What choice did I have? I was now the single mother of two, and I wanted to live." One of the most striking results of living with illness or chronic pain is realizing what was normal in the past may not be today. "Life is not what I expected, but it is still good." She shared this encouragement: "Do not keep striving for what you are to eat and what you are to drink, and do not keep worrying. For it is the nations of the world that strive after all these things, and your Father knows that you need them. Instead, strive for [God's] kingdom, and these things will be given to you as well" (Luke 12:29–31). Living your new normal may lead you to unique experiences to share with loved ones and growth opportunities you never anticipated having.

> Whether you find the idea of creating a new normal useful, you are not without hope and not without opportunities to live in a new way.

For Reflection and Discussion

1 How have you come to acceptance? If you have not, how can others help you?

2 What has been most difficult in adjusting to your or your loved one's condition?

3 What kind of planning have you done to make your new life more routine?

4 How has your faith helped you establish a new normal or new way of living?

6

What Do I Need Now?

MY HUSBAND, David, nearly died of internal bleeding before we got him to the emergency room at the local hospital. When he survived and was able to return home after just a few days, we thought his emergency was a mere bump in the road, but our ride for the next eleven years was often jarring. We weren't desperate for funds, but we spent years living in survival mode. We weren't without family or friends, but after the initial outpouring of loving support, life became pretty quiet. We weren't without information or education, but new information was hard to apply to ourselves. We weren't without counsel, but we knew how to minimize our struggles.

Both the person with the illness and the caregiver need support and help from the time of diagnosis through the long days of treatment, follow-up care, grieving losses, accepting the situation, and moving forward into new routines. We have so many questions and we long for caring people with answers. We wonder, is it reasonable to have expectations about anything, and if so, what can we anticipate? What are our options? We need information that is accessible and understandable. We want to understand what will be different and what can stay the same. We need someone in addition to medical professionals to walk with us.

We have so many questions and we long for caring people with answers.

Needed: Support and Assistance

The hospital or clinic staff, and medical care providers may make initial referrals and recommendations to the appropriate follow-up and ongoing services they know you need. Following my husband's transplant surgery, we met with a team of cross-disciplinary practitioners who were prepared to address more than the medical and pharmaceutical issues. The transplant team social worker not only helped us through a psychological assessment, she answered questions about conversations with family members, dealing with financial issues, and locating ongoing support. Menu ideas and support from the nutritionist led to a major change in our eating habits to healthier meals that resulted in better overall health. The chaplain provided us with reading materials and access to televised worship and meditation. Because our pastor was so involved with us, we did not need the services of the care-team chaplain, but it was helpful to know a pastoral-care provider was available.

Before she brought Jon home from the hospital, Sue enlisted help from her neighbors and Jon's colleagues on the police force to build an entry ramp and create a private room on the first floor for Jon, who was unable to walk and care for himself. Hospital personnel made the initial arrangements for home healthcare and gave Sue several resources for ongoing physical, social, emotional, and spiritual support. In the earliest days, when she and her children were still so overwhelmed by Jon's condition, they were able to rely on medical support from the hospital. As they grew accustomed to healthcare providers and could see for themselves what Jon needed and when, they equipped themselves with the information and tools required.

Making arrangements for the services needed may be as simple as finding someone who can give injections of medication as Jennifer did and as David and I did for a specific and limited time. In situations like Jon's and other conditions that require a range of in-home treatments and care, it may be more difficult. As long as you find someone qualified and reliable to provide the care, you can take time to breathe and meet other responsibilities. When concerned about the quality of care, or the in-home care provider is short-term, making those arrangements gets more challenging. When the skilled nurse who had developed a great relationship with Jon and his family had to leave suddenly for his own family emergency, Jon and Sue had six different people coming into their home every week for nearly three months. "It worked," Sue said. "I had to work hard to manage the schedule, but the people who helped were amazing. We know a trained health aid is best for his physical care, but those months of having family, friends, and neighbors help did wonders for his emotional growth." She told me she expects there will always be problems to solve, and sometimes she still gets overwhelmed. She has learned, however, to rely on outside assistance.

Many of us have people around us that we can count on to help us out in an emergency. When we do not know our neighbors and our family is far away, help may come from local organizations and groups, providing service to those in need. Support groups for specific illnesses and conditions actively serve many communities. You can use the internet, local library, newspapers, and telephone books to find the services you need. Faith communities and service clubs provide a variety of support. Many offer meeting rooms for support groups. Some host health fairs, medical clinics, and education programs about specific chronic conditions. Home health resources may be provided by a medical "closet," which operates like a food bank or a lending library. Periodically, we relied on a volunteer registered nurse for injections so we could avoid a daily trip to another town.

Groups and organizations in many communities have been providing meals and other help for many years. Today, those same groups can organize and provide meals using an online planner like www.mealtrain.com or www.takethemameal.com. CaringBridge also has an online organizing system, and www.carecalendar.org can be used to ensure regular ongoing assistance with errands, respite care, childcare, transportation, laundry, housecleaning, yard work, or other needs you may have. The old-fashioned way works too—get on the telephone and call the helpers and the good cooks, or send around a sign-up sheet in your group.

I cannot begin to list the books I read on chronic illness, liver disease, organ transplants, caring for a loved one, and surviving

As long as you find someone qualified and reliable to provide the care, you can take time to breathe and meet other responsibilities.

family crisis. David and I were grateful for those resources that provided insight into others' experiences and raised questions for us that we didn't know we had. Sometimes finding the answers was easy. We often returned to the medical team to clarify information for us. Reminder: You may feel alone, but you are not.

Needed: Someone to Listen

We also need people around us to love us and remind us who we are and what opportunities await us. We need people willing to listen to our story and our feelings. Who are the people we can count on? Are there people to avoid because they drag us down? Do we have someone we can call on at 2:00 a.m. when we can't sleep or are worried? We need people who will be encouraging without giving us false hope. We need people who will support us without taking over. Most of all, we need someone to listen without giving advice.

When my husband was first diagnosed, having someone who would listen to us as we told our story was very meaningful. The helpers who didn't ask questions but listened attentively with compassion as we repeated again and again all the details of the initial emergency, were gifts to us in the early days. We treasured those who listened without judgment as we poured out our "what if's," our fears of the unknown, and our anger that this had even happened in the first place. Whenever I felt God speaking directly to me, as I sensed the day David was released from the hospital—that was precious. But it was too soon and too hard for me to hear others tell me what they thought God was doing. It was the willingness of our pastor to simply be with us as we talked and cried that was helpful in those days.

Good listeners encourage both the person with the illness and their loved ones to talk through all of their questions, concerns, and responses to this major upheaval in their lives. Talking about regrets, fears, and feelings helps name and normalize concerns. Depending on the situation, another family member or friend can often be that

You may feel alone, but you are not.

helpful listener. When the loss or grief or anger leads to depression, a professional therapist may be needed. Sue and Jennifer both relied on short-term therapy to help them regain balance in their lives. Karen and Linda found support groups to be helpful and have formed several lasting relationships of mutual support. Some people share their stories of success and failures on an illness-dedicated Facebook page or blog. David and I did need people to talk to but frequently relied on each other to avoid asking for help.

Everyone needs help and support when dealing with chronic or serious illness. Although the one with the illness or pain typically gets the most attention (deservedly so), those providing care often struggle on alone and without support because, after all, they are healthy—the lucky ones. I know Mother would have welcomed and appreciated the occasional respite visitor during the days of Dad's dialysis. She left him alone only for brief trips to the grocery store across the street. After his death, she told us that she actually joyfully anticipated her weekly opportunity to walk up and down the aisles at the grocery store, "just like any other homemaker." She would have liked her shopping trips to have lasted longer, just for a chance to feel normal.

> **If you can acknowledge what you cannot do on your own, help may be available to you.**

While some of us rely on our faith in God to get us through the landmines and over every wall, others may question God's willingness to help. Others may have extended family and close friends to give us the support we seek. I don't know what it is you need, but if you can acknowledge what you cannot do on your own, help may be available to you. Ask for what you need. Some have the financial means to handle a major upheaval in employment; many do not. Connect with community and government programs that can help. Ask your neighbors to keep an eye on your house, watching for newspapers or mail piling up that indicate you may have left home in a hurry. Let them know you'd appreciate it if they could retrieve your packages until you return. Tell people you would appreciate help with meals, transportation, or errands. Ask a friend who is a good listener to drive or accompany you to appointments for testing or treatment.

Jane used her Rolodex of family and friends throughout the country to line up assistance when her family had to travel for treatments and follow-up care. Friends often had a hot meal waiting for them when they returned. No, their friends did not always think to do that on their own. Jane often had to ask, but they were happy to help whenever they could.

Needed: Spiritual Care

Whether care comes from a pastor, a health professional, a trained layperson, or a congregation member of strong faith, if your helper is a good listener, it can be life-giving. The care provider's *ability* to resolve problems, help repair relationships, or even pray isn't as crucial as someone's *willingness* to be with you. Those of us living with serious illness know that pastoral-care providers cannot fix anything, so we want companionship from someone who relies on God's strength and knows they are a helper, not a savior. The care needed is presence—a reminder of God's presence in someone who wants to understand. If ever that "nonanxious presence," as pastoral care was defined for me, is meaningful, it is for the person who will never again feel completely well. It is for the one who loves and cares for that person. Living with a loved one with chronic illness is isolating and lonely.

While pastoral care is often necessary and appreciated in times of acute illness, it may be needed more frequently and more actively when the life of a person or family is disrupted over a long period by the effects and requirements of an ongoing illness. As uncomfortable as quiet presence can be, it is the single most important thing to be offered as the helping relationship develops. Henri Nouwen's words on the difference between caring and curing are helpful. The person who is ill, in pain, fearful, angry, or anxious cannot be cured or fixed but can be helped by another's caring. Nouwen says, "The basic meaning of care is: to grieve, to experience sorrow, to cry out with."[1] Most of us prefer to give advice or act to fix whatever is broken. "Cure without care makes

> The care provider's *ability* to resolve problems, help repair relationships, or even pray isn't as crucial as someone's *willingness* to be with you.

us preoccupied with quick changes, impatient and unwilling to share each other's burden," Nouwen continues.[2]

As a seminary student, providing pastoral care for the first time, I began to understand what Nouwen was describing. When faced with fearful patients or their families seeking relief, my anxiety level rose to new heights. Learning to be, rather than to do, took time, but developing a nonanxious presence became soothing in itself. One of my best learning experiences involved a family who did not speak English and was of Hindu faith. They used their hands and eyes to ask me to stay with them. The translator, who accompanied the physician into the room to tell the family their loved one had died, talked with the family briefly. Then he turned to me and said, "They need you to be with them, to pray alongside of them, and asked that you take them to see their mother." I never said a word. When the family put on their hats and coats to leave, each person came to me with a hug and a slight bow. Being present mattered.

Chaplains and pastoral care providers are trained to be present and advised to avoid advice giving or platitude providing. They are taught to listen, and listen some more. They want to know about your condition and will listen to your stories, complaints, and concerns without judgment. They will *not* encourage you to find meaning in your suffering, but they will encourage you to find meaning in the life God has provided and continues to sustain. Compassionate spiritual support can help you see your situation as one part of life rather than allowing the illness to dictate your every thought. In a society that values production, it is so hard to maintain a sense of worth when we lose our ability to perform as we had prior to the illness. Pastors and chaplains know that as we are created in the image of God, our situation does not dictate our value. A wise pastoral care provider can help us value ourselves as we are, encouraging us to find the opportunities we may have to give as well as receive.

Even when our faith is strong and we trust God's provision for our lives, we may need spiritual care. My parents were people of faith,

> A wise pastoral care provider will *not* encourage you to find meaning in your suffering, but they will encourage you to find meaning in the life God has provided and continues to sustain.

and they could have benefited from supportive pastoral care during the long months and years of obtaining medicine, maintaining a medication schedule, adhering to a special diet, and remaining watchful for any signs of a medication reaction that could result in death. Particularly during times of crisis, a listening ear, a pastoral presence, respite support, and felt understanding would have been helpful. Maybe their desire for secrecy was so strong that any pastoral intervention would have been unwelcome. However, if those providing pastoral care understood and acknowledged how difficult receiving assistance is for those who want to keep their situation private, help may be more readily available. Empathetic pastoral-care providers will not be surprised by your feelings of embarrassment or shame and may be able to help you work through those feelings. A sense of failure or fault, or a desire to appear strong in an untenable situation by the person with the illness or by family members is not unusual to the compassionate spiritual helper.

If you are struggling with your beliefs about God's involvement or response to your illness, pastoral care can help. If you are angry, confused, or feeling abandoned by God, a pastoral care provider can help you express your feelings. The helpful pastor or chaplain may be able to help you know the love of God and God's desire for all to be well. Meeting with someone who is familiar with the love and passion of Jesus can strengthen your confidence in the spiritual and emotional healing God provides. Care providers will rely on God's strength to accompany them as they support you throughout a long-term illness, so don't be afraid to request ongoing care. Offering your own insights to a pastoral-care provider will be helpful to you and may offer new thoughts to your helper.

Care from Faith-Based Organizations

Most communities of faith pray for those who are ill and in difficult circumstances each time they gather. Some regularly offer prayers for spiritual, physical, emotional, and social healing—whatever is needed. More and more congregations are offering services of healing, creating a special service specifically focused on a particular

> Even when our faith is strong and we trust God's provision for our lives, we may need spiritual care.

person or illness. Some offer a dedicated healing service on the fifth Sunday of the month that occurs four times each year. Sometimes their services include the laying on of hands and anointing with oil. Many congregations train laypeople in healing prayer and offer prayer stations in the worship area during the celebration of Holy Communion. Ask if your church would hold a healing service for you or your loved one and ask your care providers for healing prayers. Check with family and friends if you think a service or prayers for healing might help you and your loved ones. Remember that legitimate groups do not promise physical healing but encourage a sense of wonder about the healing God does provide.

Beth and her family received healing during the healing service they attended. She described the sense of comfort and peace that had a soothing effect on all of them. A local congregation had a service for a woman diagnosed with an advanced and deadly cancer. She and her family filled three rows in the front of the church. The pastor followed the order for the Service of Healing in the Evangelical Lutheran Worship book and invited not only the woman and her husband forward for laying on of hands but her entire family and anyone in the faith community who wanted to participate. Many of the parishioners came forward to touch someone who was touching her. It was a beautiful experience for all who participated.

Local faith communities also provide a range of services that may benefit your family.

You may be able to receive home delivery of the meals some offer weekly, monthly, or on special occasions. Some churches provide transportation and respite care to individuals and families. They may also offer wellness fairs, clinics, and blood-pressure checks on a regular basis.

Needed: Self-Care

The writer of Ecclesiastes tells us, "For everything there is a season, and a time for every matter under heaven" (Eccl 3:1). Any parent of teens can tell us that the change from the season of childhood to the season of adolescence, while expected, can still generate longings for the good old days. Young couples who have established a cozy routine move into the season of parenthood and experience new love and major disruption. When the children move on to advanced schooling, careers, or marriage, we face the season many call "the empty nest." Moving from season to season brings both benefits and losses. We have seasons of joy and seasons of sorrow. There are times for service and times to care for ourselves.

If you or your loved one has just been diagnosed with a serious illness or is learning to adapt to a chronic condition, this is probably a season of self-care for you—not a time to neglect the needs of others, but time to focus first on your needs. Feeling guilty or selfish about taking care of yourself during the time when your world seems upside down and out of control is not only unnecessary, it can be debilitating to your own health and life. One avenue of self-care is recognizing that others are in their season of service and are taking care of the things you are not. Servants and caregivers are there for you as well.

Dealing with hard days is sometimes like dealing with the diagnosis in the first place. Work toward living the best life you can, remembering that sometimes, the best we can do is avoid looking

For everything there is a season, and a time for every matter under heaven.

sick or tired or in pain, creating an appearance that belies our physical or emotional distress. But when I really feel awful, I need more than lipstick or a clean shirt. You may find you get energy from dressing your best or maybe treating yourself to a day of soft pants and a favorite sweatshirt. If rituals help you, develop a new morning ritual. Create a comfortable place to enjoy your morning beverage, favorite book, music, or the view outside your window. Take a walk and pray, pouring out your pain or grief to God, or notice the gifts of God in your surroundings. Drink a tall glass of ice-cold water and enjoy eating something you love that is also healthy. Find your own tiny pleasures.

When attempting to resolve issues out of your control, asking "What can I do?" can be a question of defeat and loss of hope or it can be empowering and strengthen resiliency and hope. We may think there is nothing we can do if our only desire is to make the illness go away. But, as Stephen Hawking led my husband to believe, there is much we *can* do as we care for ourselves. Although you may want to move as quickly as possible through many of the moments in your life now, one avenue to self-care is living as well as you can in each moment. Sometimes living in the moment is just taking a breath or experiencing your feelings, but you are being intentional about living as well as possible. Each new day, each hour of the day brings both challenges and opportunities. As you care for yourself, it can be most helpful to focus on the opportunities.

Jane made greeting cards for every occasion and found peace and joy in creating just the right card for her loved ones. Karen is a basket-maker and breathes easy as she crafts. Coffee with whipping cream and just a little sweet flavoring creates a vacation mood for me that I find energizing, even when drinking decaf. I've always been jealous of people who enjoy relaxing in a bubble bath. It sounds wonderful, looks lovely, and I hate it. Maybe none of these ideas work for you. That's okay. On your next good day, give some thought to the people, places, possessions, and settings that improve your mood, and find a way to make it happen on those days when life seems just too hard.

One avenue to self-care is living as well as you can in each moment.

Asking for Help

We may need to learn how to ask for help when we know we cannot take another step on our own. And we need to accept help when it is offered. Too many times, I felt sorry for myself and my family, thinking no one really cared. I bristled at hearing of yet another benefit for a family that had so many more resources than we did. In self-pity mode, I had forgotten my brother's offer to put together a benefit concert to raise funds for our additional expenses. He called soon after David's diagnosis and genuinely wanted to be helpful. But we felt we were far too resourceful and self-sufficient to need that. "Save it for someone who really needs it," I told Mike. Even if I already knew we needed financial help, I wasn't about to accept it. It is interesting how I buried that offer in my memory when I started comparing ourselves to others. We never received a big check in the mail like some friends of ours did, but gift cards for gas and groceries appeared regularly.

If we wanted someone to help us, we had to admit needing assistance. As David and I continued to insist we were fully capable of dealing with his chronic illness, offers of help dried up. When absolutely necessary we did learn to ask, but almost always with a caveat: "If someone else is in greater need, don't worry about us." David and I strove to be the perfect family coping with illness, being the perfect patients, always encouraging helpers to aid someone who was really in need. We missed many opportunities to receive support and to allow someone else to assist us.[3] As people who generally considered ourselves to be caretakers and givers, we eventually learned that others do want to help—and they will, if given the opportunity. Comparisons are not helpful. As long as I thought we were better or worse off than someone else, I wasn't very aware of, or grateful for, the gifts and the help that came more often than I recognized at the time. David and I both needed to strengthen our ability to ask for help.

If asking for help feels too much like being weak or self-centered, consider what you might do if a friend was in your shoes. Likely, as

> We may need to learn how to ask for help when we know we cannot take another step on our own. And we need to accept help when it is offered.

a caring person, you would encourage that person to ask for help. Sometimes we just need to follow the advice we give to others. People living with their own or a loved one's illness can be strong, but our lives feel so uncertain. Be as loving and kind toward yourself as you would toward another. And think about the opportunity to give that you are offering to someone. According to my friend, Jim, "There is nothing like being able to help someone who has done so much for you." Learn to trust others to love you just as you love them. When your situation feels unbearable, you will have someone to support you.

Humor and Laughter

The illness is not funny. Pain is not funny. The situation is not funny. But . . . a sense of humor is not only helpful, it can be life-giving. Laughter is healing and helps restore perspective, manage stress, and deal with some of the worst times in our lives. An old friend, a fellow motivational speaker and trainer, always said, "Life is too serious for us to take it too seriously." Humor makes terrible situations bearable. Humor takes us outside of ourselves long enough to release endorphins, which provide a sense of well-being and provide short-term pain relief. According to the research, laughter boosts immunity, lowers stress hormones, relaxes muscles, and may even have a role in preventing heart disease. Laughter has also been shown to ease anxiety and release tension, improve mood and strengthen resilience.[4]

I first read about laughter as medicine in 1980, while preparing a series of motivational speeches. One of my well-used and appreciated lines was, "Hearty laughter is a good way to jog internally without going outdoors." It came from Norman Cousins's book *The Anatomy of Laughter*. I pulled that book out again when David was diagnosed with liver failure, thinking it could help us keep our funny bone intact. Since that time, there have been numerous scientific and anecdotal studies on the physical effects of laughter.

> Learn to trust others to love you just as you love them.

This is how my young friend Courtney takes care of herself. Her husband is fifteen years into remission from his cancer, but she now grapples with her dad's stage 4 cancer. She has a husband, two jobs, three children, and a home to maintain. Yet, she still manages to make time to see her dad and provide support to her mother. She told me, "It was hard going through this with my husband, but this is so much worse. We try to go with the flow, but his journey is so incredibly sad at times." Courtney cares for herself by honest sharing of her experiences and feelings. She recently posted this experience on her Facebook page.

> Last week my brother Travis and I took my dad to his doctor. Clearly, a doctor's appointment for someone with stage 4 cancer is pretty depressing. But, oh my goodness . . . we laughed and laughed. We laughed at ourselves. We laughed at some hilarious things the doctor said. He was awfully blunt . . . in a way that could either make you really mad, or make you crack up because he just had no filter and had no idea how rude he sounded. We all lost it in laughter after he left the room! I laugh so hard I can't breathe . . . it makes a noise that makes us laugh harder. Then my brother snorts and it all starts again! When I got home I texted my dad and said, "Sorry you had to listen to us laugh the whole time." He replied, "Your laughter was exactly what I needed." We had made his day, and he had made ours by laughing with us.

This may not be your day to read about laughter during medical treatment. Some days, we wonder if anything really is funny. Too often, it is not. But Courtney values the fun she can have with her family in the midst of a serious situation. Her post ended with these words, "Life is good for today."

Sue's family life was eased by Jon's sense of humor. The funny ways Jennifer's sons look at life give her many opportunities to laugh. My husband, David, often said, "If it's a choice between crying and laughing, I'll pick laughter every time." Roger's wife testifies to humor as a major part of his resilience during a difficult time.

The illness is not funny. Pain is not funny. The situation is not funny. But . . . a sense of humor is not only helpful, it can be life-giving. Laughter is healing and helps restore perspective, manage stress, and deal with some of the worst times in our lives.

And Proverbs 17:22 says, "A cheerful heart is a good medicine, but a downcast spirit dries up the bones." If it's funny, let's enjoy the laughter.

Not everyone is able to provide for themselves while caring for another or struggling personally with the lifestyle and pain of a chronic illness. However, as the people whose stories I've shared have discovered, self-care is possible, within a trusting understanding of human limits. When we are tired and frustrated, or frightened and confused, self-care is vital, and feels impossible.

Spiritual Journaling

Sue and Jennifer both used journaling to help them recover from depression. When Sue became seriously ill about five months after Jon's stroke, she realized she needed to take time for herself. She needed time to process what had happened, as she was so busy and preoccupied in the early months and just stifled her own feelings and needs for as long as she could. She began processing by using a journal. She recorded events, her feelings, and others' responses. Once a rebellious teenager who refused to believe in God, Sue had joined Jon's Lutheran church after they were married. As she journaled, she realized that so much of the support and assistance they had received in the earliest days had come from fellow congregation members. She began to see how God's hand was on everything that had happened and remained on all that was occurring in their lives.

There are many ways to journal, and multiple resources are available to provide direction. For many of us, journaling is a way to process our lives as they unfold and provides an outlet for our thoughts and feelings. So, you may write your prayer or a note of gratitude for answered prayer right after you record the weather report and what you wore when you went to the hospital. Each journal is as unique as the person writing it.

Proverbs 17:22 says, "A cheerful heart is a good medicine, but a downcast spirit dries up the bones."

I have always kept a daily diary, and began journaling my Bible reading time and prayers in 1976. I recorded our entire journey, beginning with the acute illness. From the first month, "We've had some good moments, but overall, life feels odd and overwhelming." A few weeks later, "These pages are so full of doom and gloom, but forcing myself to reflect, I do notice moments of joy and peace. There are times when I recognize God's presence and am grateful. Today, I give thanks for Bible study and the ladies in the study. They are amazing."

And the very next day, "Please, Jesus, please. I just want my life back. We've gotten through so much, yet I still feel so overwhelmed. Psalm 30:10 is the plea, 'Hear, O Lord and be gracious to me.' Turn my mourning into dancing." Journal keeping, recording my prayers and God's responses, played a major role in keeping my focus on God's strength and God's ability to heal.

Dorothy's Story

I was not able to talk with Dorothy, but she regularly recorded her prayers and signs of God's presence in her life. When she was diagnosed with an inoperable brain tumor, she chose to document her progress and record her prayers using a handwritten journal. She asked my sister, her dear friend, to organize and type it without correction to share with friends and family after her death. Excerpts from her journal allow me to tell her story and demonstrate how journaling might be helpful to those living with chronic or serious illness.

Dorothy wrote this: "The past days have been the most remarkable. On Tuesday, April 27, my life changed." She described her day filled with activity, including a three-mile walk, a shopping trip, a visit to a friend, some prayer-chain phone calls, a little work on a shower gift, and preparing food for dinner guests. Everything changed for Dorothy and her family when her husband asked her whether she would like a glass of wine or a cocktail. Dorothy wrote,

Selected Verses from Psalm 27

This is only a sample of the precious words I found in Psalm 27.

¹The Lord is the stronghold of my life;
of whom shall I be afraid?

⁵For he will hide me in his shelter
in the day of trouble;
he will conceal me under the cover of his tent;
he will set me high on a rock.

⁶Now my head is lifted up
above my enemies all around me . . .
I will sing and make melody to the Lord.

¹¹Teach me your way, O Lord,
and lead me on a level path
because of my enemies.
¹²Do not give me up to the will of my adversaries,
for false witnesses have risen against me,
and they are breathing out violence.

¹⁴Wait for the Lord;
be strong, and let your heart take courage;
wait for the Lord!

His question confused me and frightened me, as I suddenly couldn't comprehend what he was talking about. His response was a gift from God as he immediately took control and rushed me to St. Elizabeth's hospital. It was determined that I was having a stroke. I remember little of that next few hours. No one could understand or comprehend what I was trying to say. By early evening, my confusion was complete.

Dorothy was very ill, yet recorded her experience, thoughts, and prayers as she was able. She wrote about a nurse, led by the Holy Spirit, who asked if she could pray with Dorothy and her husband. She talked with the nurse about their encounters with

God throughout their lives and work. Dorothy trusted God for the outcomes, and returned to God's word for answers and help as she reflected day-by-day, from May 1999 to February 9, 2000, when she made her last journal entry.

In reading her journal, I expected to see the progress of her illness, and her requests for healing and an easier life. What I found was testimony to Dorothy's faith in God's ability to make anything happen. Many of her prayers were for her family and friends to know God well and to allow God to care for them. Just a few months before her death, she made this journal entry late in the afternoon:

As I jot these words, I am bathed by that "peace beyond understanding." We are momentarily waiting for a call from [the doctor]. The MRI that was taken almost a week ago was read to us by [another doctor]. Good news and "not" so good news. There have been some negative things found on the scan. God is in control. Our prayer continues that we can accept His plan for me. There is more to acceptance then thinking "Oh, well, she had a good life or, what a shame she could have traveled, done so much more etc., etc." On Christmas Eve, I was preparing myself for tears and regrets that it could be my last Christmas. Quite the opposite! I rejoiced in feeling that if I am in heaven by Christmas, I would be in a presence beyond anything I could imagine. I pray for continued strength, hope, and peace. Thank You, Thank You—Lord Jesus.

Dorothy was confused and often unable to find the right words to convey her thoughts, but her faith in God and her belief in God's abiding presence were never lost. A few sentences, taken from her last journal entries, including the last words she wrote, are encouraging.

Part of me seems as if I am so ready to go to heaven and part of me wants to be here with my family. God has shown us his power and his love as it spreads over my family. I am still so very confused. Only God knows where I am going. I am trusting that God is . . . I feel bad for the kids seeing me like this. If I am to get my strength and be able to communicate I would be so grateful. If God wants me to stay alive for some time, my prayer is that I would be able to communicate with my husband, children, and friends. God have mercy with me!

Dorothy's journals gave her a place to talk with God and a way to share both her journey and her faith with all who read her words. Sometimes she records the facts. Often, she records her feelings. And no entry is complete without a statement of faith, intercessions for others, or gratitude for God's loving grace. Her journals served her well, and, filled with evidence of God's love and presence, they became a gift to all who loved her.

You can use spiritual journaling as you read your Bible, noting specific stories and verses and how they apply to your life. A journal may also be helpful as you use the words of Scripture to create your own prayers. Claiming a word or more from the Bible can help keep us grounded and can be empowering. As you read, notice the words that give you life, and perhaps write them until you can carry them in your heart. When David was first diagnosed, I was reading through the Psalms. Psalm 27 caught not just my eye but my heart. I wrote it out in my journal several times every week until it was imprinted on my heart. Psalm 27 became the Wilke family prayer and remains my prayer today. Jane shared a special verse from the Bible (her story is shared in the next chapter). Dorothy recorded a song, based on a Bible story. My mother relied on Philippians 4:11, "For I have learned to be content with whatever I have." Karen holds on to the story of Joseph.

Whatever you choose to include your journal, you may find your writing helpful as you record, reflect, and as you pull it out later to confirm answers to prayer and moments of hope in God's love.

> For I have learned to be content with whatever I have.

> ### Praying the Scriptures
>
> The Bible is filled with prayers, and it can be helpful to rewrite them as our own prayers. Jane wrote her own prayer based on Psalm 116, A Prayer of Thanksgiving for Recovery from Illness. You may want to read through her prayer (chapter 7) or review the prayer of lament, suggested in chapter 2, before reading through these psalms. Choose one to rewrite as your own prayer: Psalm 27, 37, 42, 100, 117, 136, or find one that reflects your feelings. You can also use other stories and words from the Bible to create your prayers.

Ongoing care for yourself and your loved ones makes a big difference in the way you live with chronic or serious illness and pain. Medical and spiritual resources are available to most people without extensive travel. Other community resources I've suggested may be more available in some areas than others, but you are not alone. Individual people—pastors, health and mental-health professionals, counselors, and community volunteers—have been trained to provide the services you may need. Meet your personal needs by identifying what will be most helpful to you and seek assistance. A list of possible helping resources is provided in chapter 8, "Where Do I Find More Help?"

For Reflection and Discussion

1 How have you found the help you need to maintain your quality of life?

2 What strengths or limitations have you found in your ability to ask for what you need? How have you worked with them?

3 What spiritual practices are helpful to you?

4 What advice do you have for someone providing spiritual care in your situation?

5 What self-care practices have you identified and regularly use?

7

Is There Any Good News?

While the condition itself is not a gift or a benefit, we will see rewards.

WE MAY never be able to call our situation a gift or a blessing in disguise, and we may not want to. However, illness can lead to new learning, growth, and greater awareness of the signs of life around us. While the condition itself is not a gift or a benefit, we will see rewards. We may be able to spot them initially, in those who minister to us. Eventually, we realize how much we have learned about ourselves, our loved ones, and our community. We are able to notice the strengths and resiliency we've developed as we learned to live well in our situation.

Here are a few things I learned about myself. I learned to live in the moment, to treasure the moments. I learned to experience the pain. I learned to let go and recognize any control I thought I had was an illusion. I learned to "be there" for another, to sit quietly without my own agenda, without worrying about doing or saying the right thing. I learned that listening may be the greatest gift we can offer one another. And I learned that I will *not* learn all I need to and I will *not* always remember to live by what I have learned.

For much of my life, I fought being around people who were ill. My reaction during those last terrifying hours of being with my husband as he died led me to believe I hadn't changed. I wondered if I would even be able to complete my seminary's requirement for Clinical Pastoral Education. When I did enroll in the program, I was stunned and grateful at how well I was able to use my own experience as a spouse as I listened to the fear, the needs, and the concerns of hospital patients and their families.

My mother, who dealt with my dad's organ failure, multiple hospitalizations, drastic lifestyle change, and ultimate death, became a role model of resiliency for me when crisis hit our family. Following her example, I remained hopeful and optimistic. Sometimes I had to work at it, seeking and digging, always trying to find something of value in a bad situation. I am not a Pollyanna who sees the sunshine when the sky is overcast, but I do have fond memories of a particularly hard day becoming a special day as we changed our perspective to see with the eyes of the medical staff at the transplant clinic. We were feeling slighted, still sitting in the waiting room an hour after appointment time and frustrated that no one seemed to notice the severity of our situation. Choosing curiosity over anger, David approached the receptionist to inquire. He returned with a smile on his face. "They are finishing up a successful transplant surgery that had an unexpected twist. I hope my operation gets the same kind of attention." That day we learned that all patients are assessed upon arrival, and seen in the order of the greatest need. We did not receive the attention we wanted, but we learned that we could trust the staff to provide what was needed. We not only learned patience, we learned to be good listeners for overworked employees. Experiences like that one took us out of ourselves for a while and allowed us to "control" the good that we could find.

We Can *All* Learn

Jennifer talked about realizing her own strength while discovering just how resilient she and her children are. She discovered that struggling through such a difficult challenge forced her to seek out the positives in her life. She has learned to live and love every day, knowing that her body will continue to weaken and she may need additional surgery in the future.

Although she will never forget nearly dropping her baby when her knees gave out, she now enjoys watching that child grow and learn. The worst of Jennifer's experience occurred before her sons were old enough to understand what was happening in their family. Yet, as her boys grow, she sees the impact of her condition on them, both positive and negative. She talks with them and answers their questions to minimize the negative, and focuses primarily on their growth as interdependent and empathetic children.

"We have experienced so many beautiful moments of humanity," Sue said as she reclined in a chair near Jon, her broken leg elevated. Sue shared her feelings a few weeks after breaking her leg in two places while mowing her lawn. "I couldn't believe it. What next?" she said, and that was the last of her self-pity. Her irritability at not being able to help Jon or even herself was distracting for a time. "I didn't even want to be around myself. Everything irritated me. I even exploded at the kids one night." Sue said she fought with herself for a few days and truly hated being couch-bound. As she watched her kids set up family card games and serve the meals neighbors brought over, she gave thanks for those amazing moments of grace-filled humanity.

She also cherished the moments of hilarity. When Sue's leg had healed enough for her to drive, she loaded herself, Jon, and the kids into their van and headed to a nearby park for a family outing. She showed me the photo they took that day—Sue, sitting in a wheelchair, while Jon, Ethan, and Lauren stood around her. "Sure, breaking my leg felt like the final straw, but it helped me feel for Jon in a new and more compassionate way. Seeing Jon stand in that photo, next to me in a wheelchair, was hilarious."

Sue told me that her growth paled in comparison to that of her children. Lauren and Ethan were ages twelve and fifteen when Jon was hospitalized, so they were already taking care of themselves in many ways. The neighbors and other family members supported them during Jon's hospitalization and have done so intermittently since that time, but Lauren and Ethan also created strategies for helping their mom and dad while they cared for themselves. They know what they've lost, but neither of them would describe the past years as a time of lost childhood or adolescence. They are fully engaged in their family life and continue to enjoy relationships with friends. They meet their responsibilities for school and part-time jobs and exhibit thoughtful behavior. Both of Sue's children rapidly put their situation into perspective when friends and people they didn't even know approached them to ask for support during their own family emergencies.

"The kids are doing okay," Sue said. "They want to be helpful and they share some responsibility, but they get out, they work, they spend time with friends." Ethan signed up for football. Early each morning he got himself out of bed, hopped on his bicycle, and pedaled two miles to practice and strength training. Lauren was about to learn to drive when her dad got sick. Sue used their travel between home and hospital to give Lauren driving experience, but Lauren also relied on help from one of Jon's former colleagues. "We raised our children to be independent, self-reliant, and responsible. We had no idea this tremendous growth would occur in the midst of crisis, but they have responded so well." Sue told me that neither of her children has ever been difficult or contrary, yet she thinks their early maturity has developed as a result of Jon's condition.

Both Lauren and Ethan have a low tolerance for teenage drama. They have seen real drama up close. Sue said, "Jon's hospitalization, surgeries, and three weeks barely surviving in the Intensive Care Unit was drama enough for them." Even when Sue's children were adjusting to the huge changes in their home life, they had opportunities to realize all that they still had. They attended the funeral for a friend's mother who died of breast cancer. They sat with a friend whose dad died by suicide. According to Sue, watching their father come back to life, when others dealt with death, opened their eyes to the suffering of others. Ethan and Lauren value their family life, have developed greater compassion, and are eager to help others in difficult situations. Ethan has started high school and is enjoying freedom, fresh classroom learning, and new friends. Lauren is a senior now and plans a future career in nursing, beginning her studies at a state university within two hours of home and her family. The entire family continues to have times of great difficulty and times of great joy. In my latest conversation with Sue, she said, "We're doing well now."

We have heard for years that children are resilient, and the studies of children rebounding after personal tragedy have borne that out. Yet, their ability to put life in perspective and continue to grow in positive directions still seems amazing to their parents. Our daughter, Carli, struggled through high school while her dad was ill. Her personal dreams went unfulfilled for many years as she avoided and then struggled with the feelings she experienced. She was present at his death and was devastated by living without her father. In many ways, however, she began to heal and dream new dreams. The birth of her son, less than two years after David died, was one of her turning points. Her love for Trenten grew her capacities for empathy, and she reached out to others to share in their pain. She boldly began to represent our family in the community as her brother and I lived far away and weren't always able to get home. She visited friends and family members in the hospital, sat with grieving friends, and attended funerals, bringing love and care from us even when we could not be physically present.

A woman with the same illness as Jennifer, rheumatoid arthritis, wrote an article for the *New York Times*, describing how living with her illness affected the development of her children. She described situations that children who do not have an ill parent may not experience, including waiting for a slow-moving parent, dealing with last-minute changes in planned activities, and picking up the slack for a mom who can't complete all the tasks needed by a family. She listed situations similar to those Sue and her family experienced, ongoing events that could have been problematic without their self-awareness. The author created a list of ten positive results that arose from their negative situation. Included in her list are the development of patience, flexibility, consideration, compassion, and appreciation for service, all characteristics most parents desire for their children. Like their mother and others around her, they also learned that experiencing pain and expressing strong emotions are

> We have heard for years that children are resilient, and the studies of children rebounding after personal tragedy have borne that out. Yet, their ability to put life in perspective and continue to grow in positive directions still seems amazing to their parents.

okay. They learned that people are not defined by their abilities, nor should they be judged by appearances. She concludes her article, "Though my children would certainly prefer not to have to deal with their mom's chronic illness, there have been many gifts along this road. The growth they experienced and the lessons they learned are sticking, and for that, we are all grateful."[1]

Married people who told me about their experiences with illness and the suffering they survived also shared what they learned about marriage. One powerful foundation of their lives was the vows they made at their weddings. "In sickness and in health is real," Sue said. "It never occurred to me that our marriage would not survive. When love hurts, I rely on my vows and find strength to move forward." Even those who feared their marriages might not survive referred to their vows as a sweet reminder to stay in the struggle that was now a major part of their life. And they learned that "he's not heavy, he's my brother" is not just a song lyric but reality during those times when others might wonder, "Why don't they just collapse under the suffering?"

Linda, who selected 1 Corinthians 13 for a reading at her wedding, said it was meaningful as she and her husband made their pledge to one another. The reading ends with these words, "Faith, hope, love, these three, but the greatest of these is love." Paul's description of the blessings and benefits of love gave them an ideal to strive for throughout the years of their marriage, especially during the challenging times. "This is what I grew to count on during those painful years without a diagnosis," Linda said. Further, she told me,

> Yes, the greatest is love. But not just our human broken love. The greatest is God's love. Out of God's love, come the gifts of faith and hope. Without God's love, there would be no faith and hope. Saint Paul is not telling us what to do as much as he is describing the character of our always loving God. Knowing that made all the difference in the world.

Other married friends described living in the moment, not fretting about the future during hard times but embracing the challenge as best as they could. One of the greatest benefits of living in the moment is taking advantage of good times for intimacy, enjoying a laugh, being with family, or exploring something new—whether the calendar or clock said it was the right time for it.

Like any other facet of living with chronic or serious illness, the learning that comes is as unique as the situation. Some couples participated together in counseling or support groups and learned new ways to care for one another. Others found individual counseling to be more helpful and returned to their situation refreshed and renewed.

LuAnn is eager to talk about what she learned. She discovered praying and trusting in God's provision is bigger than she thought it was. "I was raised in the Lutheran church. I raised my kids in the Lutheran church. We went to church, said the Lord's Prayer at bedtime, and prayed before dinner. That was pretty much it." She talked about raising children in the church because it was the right thing to do. She said she learned the prayers and taught them to her children. "It was for them," she said, about ensuring her children went to Sunday school and were confirmed into the Lutheran faith. "When I got sick," LuAnn told me, "I started to pray, really pray." That's not so unusual. People often pray when they are in trouble. But LuAnn was changed forever by her beginning attempts at prayer.

When LuAnn's prayers did not yield the results she wanted, she realized she had more to learn. Like Linda and others who suffer as they wait for a diagnosis, LuAnn asked the questions, "Where are you, God? Why isn't anything changing? Aren't you going to fix this?" Her son was going to be married soon, and at that time she was in no condition to attend the wedding. The mother of the groom would be noticeably absent. Several events helped her learn the difference between her immediate desire and God's timing.

One of the greatest benefits of living in the moment is taking advantage of good times for intimacy, enjoying a laugh, being with family, or exploring something new—whether the calendar or clock said it was the right time for it.

Part of God's healing process for LuAnn included getting her to a physician who could diagnosis her condition and begin treatment. She was learning to wait for God and wondered if another three-hour trip to a doctor who probably wouldn't know what was wrong with her was really her next step. Both her children and her husband provided God's answer by getting her into the family car and driving her to the appointment, where both her physical and her spiritual life were transformed.

LuAnn was determined to rely on God, yet learned that she needed to know God better so she would be better prepared for the different ways God acted in her life. Her developing prayer life grew into Bible reading and times of silence and solitude in God's presence. She learned that God does not leap into our lives with miraculous answers on our timelines. She learned to look for God in everything that she experienced, and she was not disappointed. Her illness will not be cured. She will never be completely symptom free. Her new normal is often frustrating, but she gives thanks daily for her children and for her husband's attentiveness and care. "Hope is not built on church attendance and memorized prayers. It is built on faith and trust in a God who is bigger than we expect," LuAnn stated with confidence.

Whether we learn more about ourselves or our loved ones, discover positive characteristics in the world around us, or develop a greater capacity for faith or compassion, it is possible to find value in our experience with chronic or serious illness. On those days when I felt at the end of my rope and had no desire to hang on, I asked God to help me learn from the situation. Too often, the learning hurts, but ultimately, we find something to cherish.

Sharing the Experience

Talking about our struggles and successes with demanding and difficult situations comes easily to some and is nearly impossible for others. Although temperament and desire for privacy may make it challenging, telling our story can be helpful to others and to

> Whether we learn more about ourselves or our loved ones, discover positive characteristics in the world around us, or develop a greater capacity for faith or compassion, it is possible to find value in our experience with chronic or serious illness.

ourselves. One of the things I admired about my parents when Dad was hospitalized multiple times after his kidney failure was their ability to reach out to others with their own story. After years of keeping Dad's diabetes secret, they learned that talking with others in similar situations was helpful. Even the young healthy couple who provided housing for them when they needed to stay near the hospital grew through their experience with my parents. When Pete and Pam faced their own suffering, they met their hardships with a faith borne out of witnessing my mother and father during crisis.

Years before my husband's illness changed our lives, I heard Joni Eareckson Tada speaking on a radio program. I had been struggling with a personal concern and appreciated her upbeat approach to resolving difficult issues. One sentence stood out for me: "A witness is always stronger when it comes out of personal experience." As you find ways to live with hope, parts of your story may be beneficial to others. People are encouraged by vulnerability and willingness to talk about those things that cause us pain. Not everyone is at a point where they are able to do this, but, if and when you get there, know that if you choose to share your story, it can bring hope and healing to another. Something for you to keep in mind as you think about sharing your experience with others: This illness of yours or a family member did not happen so you would be able to listen and talk to others about their situation. Rather, being able to share your experience is an act of God's redemption. God takes an awful situation and uses it to support someone else in similar circumstances. I believe that was what Joni was saying during her radio broadcast.

As David was recovering from his liver transplant surgery, I was certain God had a plan for us to share our experience. At the time, I thought we would give presentations on liver disease and the importance of organ donations. Later, I believed we were to provide comfort and support to anyone experiencing a serious illness or surgery. We did neither of those intentionally, but our shared experience did impact others. After he died, so many friends and people in our community told me how much they learned about

> As you find ways to live with hope, parts of your story may be beneficial to others.

marriage by watching David and me navigate the ups and downs of his illness and recovery. Their comments came as a great surprise to me, as I thought we had done nothing as a couple to share all that we had learned. God's redemption of bad situations does not always come in ways we expect, but it comes and gives us hope.

I marvel at the rapid connections people living with illness are able to make with one another when we realize we have a shared struggle. Many of the resources I consulted while writing this book identified a common question asked by people living with illness or pain: "Why didn't anyone tell me it would be like this?" When we share parts of our experience, we help others understand how their lives may change. Whether we are just beginning to make a life that includes illness and pain or we have already found new ways to thrive, connecting with others who have experienced or are currently experiencing something similar is life-enhancing. As Sue shared quotes from Facebook and the blogs she regularly read, she told me her response to the postings: "They made it through. We can do this too."

Jennifer shared her experience in another way. When her physician failed to give credence to her post-surgical concerns, resulting in another surgery and compartment disease, she decided to go public. She sued her orthopedic surgeon to ensure others didn't go through her experience. "When my case was settled," she told me, "I knew others would be spared, and that meant more to me than the money I used for medical bills." Her attorney told her the lawsuit led the physician and his clinic to change their procedures when future patients showed the symptoms Jennifer displayed. "I was uncomfortable with the lawsuit, but I am proud that my efforts will have a positive impact on future patients," she said.

By sharing our own stories, we can share our hope with others. Jane kept friends and family informed about their life through the CaringBridge website, described in chapter 5. As Jane wrote, she shared not only medical updates and treatment results but her story of faith and hope. I met Jane when her husband and I were

> God's redemption of bad situations does not always come in ways we expect, but it comes and gives us hope.

> By sharing our own stories, we can share our hope with others.

seminary classmates. She had recently completed treatment for breast cancer and was eager to be part of the seminary community. She smiled and spoke with everyone she met and served as the seminary's receptionist during Brian's years of study. She and Brian had survived their experience with serious illness and were moving forward. She served great meals, shared her special brownie recipe, and hosted game nights for Brian's classmates. Her appreciation for life and her love for God were obvious in everything she said and did. We saw each other several times after graduation and kept in touch through Facebook. The news that she was fighting cancer again was shocking and sad to all who loved her and Brian.

Jane's Story

While Jane's journals remain private, her family allowed me to share excerpts from CaringBridge to convey the authenticity, courage, and hope that carried Jane through her illness. This may be difficult to read, as Jane did not survive her illness, but her joy in living and bright faith shine through the following entries. Still reeling from the news that cancer had returned in her bones, she posted this note of thanksgiving the day following the new diagnosis:

> Thanks to everyone for all the encouragement and prayers. So great to hear from friends far and near, old and new. Your notes lift my spirit. And for those who are near, have no fear, we will let you know if you can help in any way. We learned the first go around to be open to the blessings others wanted to offer.

She was gracious and grateful enough to thank family and friends, and humble enough to acknowledge her family would need help. She also shared updates that showed her confidence in God's willingness to answer prayer and invited friends to continue praying for her family as well. She shared her feelings about the physical pain she experienced, and she shared her joy in celebrating special occasions with friends and family. Two years into her treatment, Jane wrote this on CaringBridge:

> This last week started with a great sermon on not letting fear
> control your life delivered by that special (yes, I'm biased) pastor
> at Le Sueur and Vista parish and then a Prayer Service of Healing
> for me led by Pastor Scott, including anointing with oil blessing by
> our retired Pastor Espe. Inspiration from Pastor Scott and beautiful
> blessing from Pastor Espe. Such an amazing group of friends here
> who took time from their Sunday afternoon to attend and surround
> Brian, Josh, and me (and Jessica) in prayer and share the peace. The
> Spirit was at work in that space. These events reminded me to keep
> my trust in God as the healer, and I've come back to that thought a
> lot in the last couple of days.

Jane was to depend on God's healing throughout her journey.
Because CaringBridge allows for responses, Jane was showered with
words of love and encouragement and assured of continuing prayers.
But she gave even better than she received. Her posts were often
filled with gratitude and praise for the medical personnel caring for
her, for the parishioners and neighbors who provided transportation
and meals for her family, and for the strength she received through
Bible reading. Jane told her story honestly and expressed feelings
many may share:

> I think I've said this before but being a cancer patient is a bit like
> being on a roller coaster. You never know what bumps are ahead . . .
> The oncologist thinks the cancer may have adapted itself to the
> chemo I'm on and it may be time to try a different drug but to go
> ahead and start . . . So, I have to admit I felt a bit blue after hearing
> that the cancer antigen is up a bit . . . But, now after resting for a
> few hours I'm feeling more up and looking forward to the days
> ahead. Thanks everyone for your prayers . . . I'm just going to pray
> for a good scan and wise doctors to figure out the next approach, if
> needed. God will take care of that and so much more. God's got a
> great track record.

Jane posted regularly throughout her treatment and often
shared how she remained aware of God's presence with her. She

commented on the loud noise of the MRI machine, telling how she survived it:

> I usually concentrate on my healing verse, but all this week and that morning especially I've had the refrain of the hymn "Blest Are They" running through my mind . . . "Rejoice and be glad! Blessed are you, holy are you! Rejoice and be glad! Yours is the kingdom of God!"

Jane talked about feeling especially blessed the day of her MRI. Her friend Karen had picked her up and spent the entire morning keeping her company and then waiting for the hour-long scan. Whether she was feeling ill or having a good day, Jane's appreciation for those who helped her never wavered. She remained welcoming and grace-filled even when her body wanted to quit. Jane posted:

> My cup runneth over this week! I wish everyone could feel so loved and cared for. So, you may have an idea now of why that refrain keeps running through my mind. Because of all these blessings, I remain positive and determined to beat the odds once again. Regardless of the outcome, I know God is with us and has planted each of us in just the right place.

Even as Jane's illness worsened, she retained her positive attitude, writing, "I'm certainly not ready to give up. I think the oncologist wonders if I understand the situation. So, asking for prayers for next treatment plan and for Brian, Jess, and Josh, too. Each day is a gift, hope you all are enjoying this one." That was one of Jane's last posts to CaringBridge. Brian wrote two more and then this one appeared: "Jane passed into our Lord's loving and waiting embrace early this afternoon at home. She had been still and (finally) resting peacefully since last night." He closed with words of gratitude and his sentiment of blessing to all readers.

Theirs was a difficult and grief-filled journey that God's abiding presence enabled them to move through with love and grace. Jane left many words, projects, and expressions of her faith, maybe none so beautiful as her personal rendition of Psalm 116, written as she ended her breast cancer treatment, and read at her funeral and burial and posted at CaringBridge:

> I love God because he has heard my prayers. Because He listened to me, I will call on Him all my life.
> The traps of illness overcame me. The pain of surgery and cancer took its toll; I suffered chemo and radiation.
> I called upon God, "Hold me in your loving arms!"
> Gracious is God and bountiful. Our God is merciful. He provides for the sick; when I was low, He cared for me.
> Return, my spirit, to the stillness, for God continues to care.
> God continues to bless my life with a loving family. My family is blessed with gracious friends. Our souls are tended in a Christian community.
> My faith grew when my body was weakest. I asked, "Why *not* me?"
> What shall I return to God for all He's done for me? I will witness to the goodness of God. I will pay His love and bounty forward.
> Precious is God to me and my family. God, I am Yours, I will strive to do Your will. I offer myself as a disciple and will continue to call on Your help.
> I will spend time in Your presence and listen to Your voice. Praise the LORD!

Jane left behind a throng of people influenced and blessed by her life. From the recipients of her crafted greeting cards to the teenager who carried her groceries to the car, all who knew Jane were changed by her joy and her grace. I pray her story encourages you to know God's never-ending love for you. In sharing her experience, Jane's story changed lives.

Sharing our story can not only ease our own hurt, it can give hope to others. We need one another to survive and thrive. You may remain unconvinced and that's okay. There are others willing to talk about their struggles and there will always be opportunities for you to share if you choose.

We need one another to survive and thrive.

Finding Meaning

There is nothing inherently good about illness or struggling to live with pain, yet most of us seek meaning in what has happened in our lives. Looking for the purpose or meaning in our situation leads us back to asking Why? or What is the reason for this? Even when we learn, develop gratitude, grow in our faith, or locate nuggets of joy in our situation, we may still struggle to find meaning.

Some of us look to God's action in our life, as we live, to find meaning and purpose. To be able to point to God's miracles and spiritual healing gives purpose and hope to those who may once have felt hopeless. Struggling with why some are healed physically and others are not, and why some have multiple complications and others find a way to thrive without physical healing, is painful and fruitless. Chronic or serious illness or pain reminds us that we are human and are dependent upon the grace of others and on God's grace. Karen found meaning in these words: "Therefore I am content with weaknesses, insults, hardships, persecutions, and calamities for the sake of Christ; for whenever I am weak, then I am strong" (2 Cor 12:10).

The truth is that Christ's power can show through our weaknesses, but it remains difficult to find meaning in a life-threatening or lengthy illness. I trust God's love can and will redeem any situation, but my search for meaning came from a number of different places, including Lamentations 3. Although the book of Lamentations was created in response to the destruction of Jerusalem and the accompanying events, this powerful writing seems to encompass the laments of someone who feels persecuted by chronic illness. The author is grieving his own captivity and torture.

If you feel like you are being held captive by a chronic or serious illness and distressed by the disease or the ramifications of the condition, this could be your cry to God. The third chapter of Lamentations gives us honest words to describe our pain and address issues we do not want to accept. It isn't easy being honest about our

> Even when we learn, develop gratitude, grow in our faith, or locate nuggets of joy in our situation, we may still struggle to find meaning.

Cries of Lamentation

These words selected from Lamentations 3 can offer hope to those grappling with illness.

The Lord is good to those who wait for him,
    to the soul that seeks him.
It is good that one should wait quietly
    for the salvation of the Lord. (vv. 25–26)

For the Lord will not
    reject forever.
Although he causes grief, he will have compassion
    according to the abundance of his steadfast love;
for he does not willingly afflict
    or grieve anyone. (vv. 31–33)

I called on your name, O Lord,
    from the depths of the pit;
you heard my plea, "Do not close your ear
    to my cry for help, but give me relief!"
You came near when I called on you;
    you said, "Do not fear!"
You have taken up my cause. (vv. 55–58)

feelings, especially if we are angry at God or blaming God for our situation. The good news is, God already knows how we feel. God is not surprised and certainly not undermined by our honest feelings. Expressing them out loud or writing our lament in a journal invites God to respond. (See chapter 2 for a sample lament.)

You may not be prepared to rail at God as you look for purpose, but these words can encourage us to remain hope-filled when God does not provide what we so desperately long for. Lamentations 3 begins, "I have seen affliction . . ." The turning point comes after twenty verses and continues, "But this I call to mind and therefore I have hope: The steadfast love of the Lord never ceases, his mercies never come to an end; they are new every morning; great is your faithfulness. 'The Lord is my portion,' says my soul, 'therefore I will hope in him'" (Lam 3:21–24). As I sought purpose in our life, these words reminded me that God's steadfast love endures. Even when we can't feel it, even when it seems God is nowhere involved. God's steadfast love endures. God's mercies never end. God's faithfulness is beyond all imagining. And that is our hope.

Many of us have been told stories about people being healed because of strong faith. Yes, Jesus commended those with faith. He also healed those without seeing any evidence of faith. And many faithful people were not healed. "If your faith was strong enough," a fellow church member told my mother, "Your husband would be healed." Can it get any more hurtful than that, especially when you are already questioning your own faith? We already have so many questions, so many fears and worries, we don't need those questions or comments. Our faith in God's mercy and love comforts us, gives us courage, and reminds us that God is so much more than we can imagine. We can trust that God does want health and wholeness for

True Beauty

Sue recently posted a picture of a mended broken bowl accompanied by this comment: "Instead of the break diminishing the bowl's appeal, a new sense of its vitality and resilience raised appreciation to even greater heights. The bowl has become more beautiful for having been broken. The true life of the bowl began the minute it was dropped." Sue commented on her own post:

> Today is the 2nd year anniversary of Jon's brain injury. I don't think I could have said it any better than the quote above. We have picked up the pieces of our lives and mended them back together with the bits of gold around us. The broken parts remain visible, but the beautiful repair and history it shows, make it priceless. "The true life of the bowl began the minute it was dropped" . . . beautiful words on a milestone day.

each one of us, and God's faithfulness does not necessarily lead to a cure or the resolution we are seeking.

Meaning comes when we recognize that we may be helpless to change our situation, but we can be hopeful in light of God's unfailing love. The entire eighth chapter of Romans is helpful to me and I appreciate the following three verses: "We know that all things work together for good for those who love God, who are called according to his purpose" (v. 28). And, "No, in all these things we are more than conquerors through him who loved us. For I am convinced that neither death, nor life, nor angels, nor rulers, nor things present, nor things to come, nor powers, nor height, nor depth, nor anything else in all creation, will be able to separate us from the love of God in Christ Jesus our Lord" (vv. 38–39). Whichever words of God or experiences are meaningful to us, we can trust the assurance of God's loving care throughout our struggles.

Seeking God's Reassurance

Having someone with deep faith as a support person or care provider can help us focus on God's loving power in our lives. Invite a faith-filled friend or a pastoral-care provider to walk with you through words from Scripture that could be helpful to you. I found strength and healing in the following verses:

- Jesus said, "As the Father has loved me, so I have loved you; abide in my love" (John 15:9). Jesus wants us to remain close; Jesus wants us to find healing and wellness in him. The power of God's Holy Spirit can help us cling to the love of Jesus.
- Jesus calls us, "Come to me, all you that are weary and are carrying heavy burdens, and I will give you rest" (Matt 11:28). We can go to Jesus, not to fix things, but to connect with the source of all that is good, loving, and healing. Healing prayer renews our relationship with God.
- Jesus continues, "Take my yoke upon you, and learn from me; for I am gentle and humble in heart, and you will find rest for your souls. For my yoke is easy, and my burden is light" (vv. 29–30). Jesus invites us to share our burden in relationship with him.
- Although his life did not always show his belief and he encountered great loss, the psalmist David rejoiced in God's everlasting love with these words: "For great is your love, reaching to the heavens; your faithfulness reaches to the skies" (Ps 57:10).

God's Got This

I want so earnestly to give you just what you need, to point you to the person, place, resource that will improve the quality of your life. Unfortunately, I know what doesn't work for me, but I don't know what works or doesn't work for you. I know this: it feels horrible to be ill, it feels horrible to love someone who is ill, and it feels horrible when no one can make it better.

I want to give you a happy ending. I want to give you a sense of meaning and purpose and desire for being alive, and I can't do that. My ideas, suggestions and lists of activities, books and other resources are just that—mine. I invite you to join me in acknowledging that only God can provide what is truly needed, what is genuinely helpful, and what is long-lasting. What you may need more than anything else is to know God is present with you and that God does listen. Hear God speak to your heart—to answer your deepest longings, to hold you close as you tremble with fear, explode with rage, burst into tears that won't stop. God is with you now and always.

Some moments, some days, sometimes God gives *us* the strength we need to feel the pain. Other times *God's* strength needs to be enough. And often, more often than we can see, God lifts us up and out and over or through and leads us to a person, a place, a resource, an idea that renews our purpose and a desire to be alive in all things.

For Reflection and Discussion

1 How might you discover all that you have learned from your experience?

2 How does your experience contribute to your development as a spouse, family member, or friend?

3 Identify those parts of your story that might benefit others. How could you share just those parts of your experience?

> Hear God speak to your heart—to answer your deepest longings, to hold you close as you tremble with fear, explode with rage, burst into tears that won't stop. God is with you now and always.

The following lyrics of "The Anchor Holds" still come to mind as frequently today as they did through David's illness and the aftermath of his death.

The Anchor Holds

Words and music by Lawrence Chewning and Ray Boltz

I have journeyed through the long dark night
Out on the open sea
By faith alone
Sight unknown
And yet His eyes were watching me
The anchor holds though the ship is battered
The anchor holds though the sails are torn
I have fallen on my knees
As I faced the raging seas
The anchor holds in spite of the storm
I've had visions
I've had dreams
I've even held them in my hand
But I never knew they would slip right through
Like they were only grains of sand
Chorus
I have been young but I am older now
And there has been beauty these eyes have seen
But it was in the night
Through the storms of my life
Oh, that's where God proved His love to me[2]

4 What role has your faith played in your learning and your willingness to talk about your journey with others?

5 What questions and concerns remain? How might you live with the questions or find answers that help?

6 What stories, books, verses, and songs have been helpful to you?

8

Where Do I Find More Help?

Resources

Books on Chronic Illness, Pain, and Invisible Illnesses

Bernhard, Toni. *How to Live Well with Chronic Pain and Illness: A Mindful Guide*. Somerville, MA: Wisdom Publications, 2015.

- A guide to living well, this resource includes strategies for self-care and tips on dealing with medical professionals and other service providers. The underlying theme is *caring attention* toward the illness or pain, which the author derived from Buddhist practices.

Rosenfeld, Arthur. *The Truth about Chronic Pain: Patients and Professionals on How to Face It, Understand It, Overcome It*. New York: Basic, 2004.

- This book is divided into three sections, each written by a different group of authors: Patients in Pain, Caregivers on Pain, and Thinkers about Pain. Rosenfeld's slant on the subject is clear: no one should suffer from pain.

Selak, Joy H., and Steven S. Overman, MD. *You Don't Look Sick: Living Well with Chronic Invisible Illness*. New York: Demos Health, 2012.

- This practical resource details Selak's life of chronic invisible illness, including many of the concerns those living with chronic illness share. Writing the book with a physician enabled the author to provide sound medical responses to her illness.

Wright, H. Norman. *Coping with Chronic Illness*. Eugene, OR: Harvest House, 2010.

- This book begins by describing the epidemic that is chronic illness and walks the reader through the steps necessary for survival. It includes information on both the fight for diagnosis and the challenges of having an invisible illness with rapidly fluctuating symptoms.

Books for Inspiration and Spiritual Support

Briehl, Susan, and Marty Haugen. *Turn My Heart*. Chicago: GIA Publications, 2003.

- This book contains essays, songs, poems, and prayers for those seeking healing and hope.

Nepo, Mark. *Inside the Miracle: Enduring Suffering, Approaching Wholeness*. Boulder, CO: Sounds True, 2015.

- If we had Mark Nepo's gift of prose and poetry, any one of us may have written this book. It tells the story of his journey as a human being living with cancer. Much of the book is pulled from the journals he has kept during his life and is filled with our questions and his ideas about God's answers.

Nouwen, Henri J. M. *Here and Now: Living in the Spirit*. New York: Crossroad, 1994.

- Nouwen's own struggles and his compassion for others are reflected in this little book of meditations about the gains in losses, the joys in struggles, and the difficulties and rewards of prayer, among other topics.

———. *The Inner Voice of Love: A Journey Through Anguish to Freedom*. New York: Doubleday, 1998.

- More spiritual inspiration from Henri Nouwen, this volume contains sixty-four brief essays on trusting God's love in all aspects of your journey. There is a meditation for many of the concerns that trouble those living with illness.

Oates, Wayne E. *Nurturing Silence in a Noisy Heart: How to Find Inner Peace*. Minneapolis: Augsburg Fortress, 1996.

- This little book accompanied me to my husband's treatments, appointments, laboratory testing, and emergency hospitalizations. It was the first book I picked up after his death in 2006.

Wakefield, James L. *Sacred Listening: Discovering the Spiritual Exercises of Ignatius Loyola*. Grand Rapids: Baker, 2006.

- In addition to a chapter explaining spiritual journaling, this resource contains essays, prayers, and strategies for listening to God and helping others listen to God. This book may be used individually, with a partner, or in a group.

Whitcomb, Holly W. *Seven Spiritual Gifts of Waiting*. Minneapolis: Augsburg Fortress, 2005.

- Waiting for anything can be difficult. If we refocus our thoughts when waiting, we may reap the seven spiritual benefits Whitcomb details in this book.

Williams, Bill. *Naked Before God: The Return of the Broken Disciple*. Harrisburg, PA: Morehouse, 1998.

- Taking on the persona of one Jesus's disciples, Williams describes his lifelong battle with cystic fibrosis. Once active in the world of technology, Bill graduated from the Lutheran School of Theology at Chicago and served a congregation in Texas for one year. He died soon after this book was published. It is a challenging read, but full of Williams's theology of suffering.

Wolfelt, Alan D. *Understanding Your Grief.* Fort Collins, CO: Companion Press, 2003.

- This publication of the Center for Loss and Life Transition rejects the myths surrounding grief and offers strategies and journaling ideas to help individuals accomplish the difficult work of grieving.

Locating and Using Local and Regional Resources

Your physician will refer you to the medical resources you need and may be able to help you make other connections as well. As previously suggested, ask professionals, neighbors, friends, and family members for their recommendations and referrals when seeking outside assistance. Your local news media, library, service clubs, churches, telephone directories, community magazines, and word of mouth are all useful in obtaining needed resources. Your life now includes an aspect perhaps unknown to you previously and you may think you do not know where to find the help you need. Once you begin looking, however, you may be surprised by how much help is readily available in your own or neighboring communities.

Locating and Using Online Resources

If you are unaware of local resources to meet your needs, you may want to use online resources. Using your chosen web browser, type in the name of your illness. The first results will usually include the national association for that disease, illness, or condition. For example, I searched for resources related to ALS and found: Amyotrophic Lateral Sclerosis—The ALS Association.

If you are searching for information about chronic pain, type "chronic pain" into the search field of your web browser. When I searched for chronic pain, the first result was an advertisement for a therapy. Skip that one. The second result was WebMD. Obtain your physician's recommendation regarding online medical resources.

The third result? I hit pay dirt, an online article, "Chronic Pain: Symptoms, Diagnosis & Treatment," found at medlineplus.gov. I am inclined to trust .gov sites.

Local and regional resources may also be found using your web browser. Type in the kind of resource you are seeking. When I entered "home healthcare," the first six responses were advertisements for healthcare services, followed by a map and additional information for local area home healthcare providers. The next several results were .gov listings, followed by additional local resources. I found a similar pattern of results for "respite care," "disability assistance," and "grocery delivery."

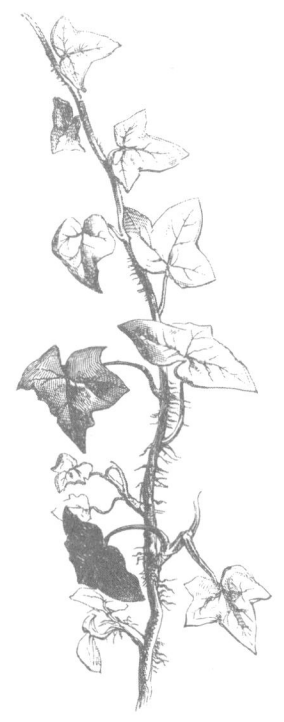

Notes

Chapter 1: What Is the Diagnosis?

1. Patricia F. Adams, Whitney K. Kirzinger, and Michael E. Martinez, *Summary Health Statistics for the US Population: National Health Interview Survey*, 2012, National Center for Health Statistics, *Vital and Health Statistics* 10, no. 259 (December 2013): https://tinyurl.com/y9svf9tu.
2. "Chronic Pain," American Chronic Pain Association, https://tinyurl.com/y8pb8xbo.
3. He asked that his identity not be disclosed.
4. Joni Eareckson Tada, "Purpose in the Pain: An Interview with Joni Eareckson Tada," *Tabletalk* October 1, 2011, https://tinyurl.com/ya445apt.
5. Joni Eareckson Tada and Joe Musser, *Joni: An Unforgettable Story* (Grand Rapids: Zondervan, 2001).
6. Banding involved surgically placing tiny rubbery bands around enlarged veins in David's esophagus so they would not bleed.

Chapter 2: Why Do I Feel Like This?

1. David Kessler, "A Message from David Kessler," Grief.com, https://tinyurl.com/ya6gktbr..
2. Henri J. M. Nouwen, *The Road to Daybreak* (New York: Doubleday, 1988), 105.
3. Genevieve Davis Ginsberg, *Widow to Widow* (Cambridge, MA: DeCapo, 1997).
4. NIH Publication No. 15-MH–8015, by the National Institute of Mental Health US Department of Health and Human Services.
5. Veronique Mead, *The Chronic Illness and Trauma Connection* (N.p.: Chronic Illness Trauma Studies, 2017).

Chapter 3: What Challenges Will I Face?

1. Paul J. Donoghue and Mary E. Siegel, *Sick and Tired of Feeling Sick and Tired: Living with Invisible Chronic Illness* (New York: W. W. Norton, Kindle Edition, 2000), 5–6.

Chapter 4: What If the Patient Is My Child?

1. A. L. Quittner, L. Goldbeck, J. Abbott, et al., "Prevalence of Depression and Anxiety in Patients with Cystic Fibrosis and Parent Caregivers: Results of the International Depression Epidemiological Study across Nine Countries," *Thorax* 69 (2014): 1090–97.
2. Mindy Viering, "10 Ways to Cope with a Child's Chronic Illness," Parenting, https://tinyurl.com/ycz347kn.
3. Janneke Hatzmann, Niels Peek, Hugo Heymans, Heleen Maurice-Stam, and Martha Grootenhuis, "Consequences of Caring for a Child with a Chronic Disease: Employment and Leisure Time of Parents," *Journal of Child Health Care* 18, no. 4 (2014): 346–57.
4. Elizabeth Leis-Newman, "Caring for Chronically Ill Kids," *Monitor on Psychology* 42, no. 3 (2011): 36.

Chapter 5: What Can I Control?

1. Reinhold Niebuhr, "Serenity Prayer," BeliefNet.com, https://tinyurl.com/y9xgjdjb. Trevor Hudson, author of *The Serenity Prayer: A Simple Prayer to Enrich Your Life* (Nashville: Upper Room Books, 2012), has exhaustively researched the origins of this prayer and explains his findings in "The Story Behind the Serenity Prayer," an introduction to his book. He states: "With regard to its authorship, no one can tell for sure who wrote it! . . . What we do know is that its opening lines were used by Reinhold Niebuhr (1892–1971), a Protestant theologian who lectured for several years at the Union Theological Seminary in New York, at the beginning of a chapel address he gave in 1934."
2. CaringBridge is a free online site for those who are ill and their families to broadly share updates without making numerous telephone calls or sending letters. Family and friends are encouraged to respond to the updates so communications can

be shared. Learn more about CaringBridge at www.caring bridge.org.

3. I found some interesting explanations at "Origin of 'The New Normal' as a Freestanding Phrase," English Language and Usage, StackExchange, https://tinyurl.com/y7n89zxm.

Chapter 6: What Do I Need Now?

1. Henri J. M. Nouwen, *Out of Solitude* (Notre Dame: Ava Maria, 1984), 34.
2. Nouwen, *Out of Solitude*, 36.
3. Some lessons need to be repeated. Recalling David's last infection, the one that took his life, I remember being urged by friends and family to call our pastor for support. I didn't recognize the seriousness of the situation, and I knew there were others in our congregation who needed pastoral support. Our independence and belief in the picture we had created of ourselves deprived us of some much-needed spiritual strength and support at a time when that very thing was crucial.
4. This link will take you to an easy-to-read guide to the impact of laughter on illness: "Laughter is the Best Medicine," HelpGuide.org, https://tinyurl.com/y727l8td.
Note the disclaimer at the bottom of the webpage: The content of this reprint is for informational purposes only and NOT a substitute for professional advice, diagnosis, or treatment.

Chapter 7: Is There Any Good News?

1. Paula M. Fitzgibbons, "10 Things My Chronic Illness Taught My Children," *New York Times*, August 16, 2017.
2. © 1994 Shepherd Boy Music/ASCAP, used by permission.

Bibliography

American Chronic Pain Association theapca.org.

CaringBridge, caringbridge.org.

Chronic Illness Trauma Studies. chronicillnesstraumastudies.com.

Donoghue, Paul J., and Mary E. Siegel. *Sick and Tired of Feeling Sick and Tired: Living with Invisible Chronic Illness.* Kindle edition. New York: W. W. Norton, 2000.

Ginsburg, Genevieve Davis. *Widow to Widow.* Cambridge, MA: DeCapo, 1997.

Hatzmann, Janneke, Neils Peek, Hugo Heymans, Heleen Maurice-Stam, and Martha Grootenhuis. "Consequences of Caring for a Child with a Chronic Disease: Employment and Leisure Time of Parents." *Journal of Child Health Care* 18, no. 4 (2014): 346–57.

Kübler-Ross, Elisabeth. *On Life after Death.* Berkeley, CA Celestial Arts, 2004.

Leis-Newman, Elizabeth. "Caring for Chronically Ill Kids." *Monitor on Psychology* 42, no. 3 (2011).

National Center for Health Statistics. cdc.gov.

National Institute of Mental Health. US Department of Health and Human Services. www.nimh.nih.gov.

Niebuhr, Reinhold. "The Serenity Prayer." beliefnet.com. https://tinyurl.com/y9xgjdjb.

Nouwen, Henri J. M. *Out of Solitude.* Notre Dame: Ava Maria, 1984.

———. *The Road to Daybreak*. New York: Doubleday, 1988.

Quittner, A. L., L. Goldbeck, J. Abbott, et al. "Prevalence of Depression and Anxiety in Patients with Cystic Fibrosis and Parent Caregivers: Results of The International Depression Epidemiological Study across Nine Countries," *Thorax* 69 (2014).

Stages of Grief. grief.com.

Tada, Joni Eareckson. "Purpose in the Pain: An Interview with Joni Eareckson Tada," *Tabletalk*, October 1, 2011, https://tinyurl.com/ya445apt.

Tada, Joni Eareckson, and Joe Musser. *Joni: An Unforgettable Story*. Grand Rapids: Zondervan, 2001.

Viering, Mindy. "10 Ways to Cope with a Child's Chronic Illness." Parenting, https://tinyurl.com/ycz347kn.

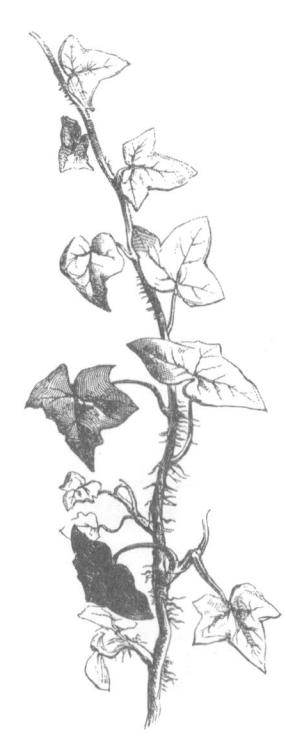